MISSISSIPPI
Hometown Cookbook

MISSISSIPPI
Hometown Cookbook

by Sheila Simmons and Kent Whitaker

Great American Publishers
www.GreatAmericanPublishers.com

TOLL-FREE 1.888.854.5954

Great American Publishers

171 Lone Pine Church Road • Lena, MS 39094
1.888.854.5954 • www.GreatAmericanPublishers.com

ISBN 978-1-934817-08-7 (1-934817-08-2)

10 9 8 7 6 5 4

by Sheila Simmons & Kent Whitaker

Front cover photos: Monmouth: Find your true south at Monmouth Plantation in Natchez, Mississippi by visiting monmouthplantation.com. Member, Small Luxury Hotels of the World and Historic Hotels of America • Magnolia © Earl Eliason • Crossroads © Coahoma County Tourism, visitclarksdale.com • Food: StockFood © Glenn Peterson

Back cover photos Food: © Kimbery Johnson image from bigstockphoto.com • Captain Catfish © World Catfish Festival

Inside photos: • from istockphoto.com: • Appetizers p9 © Jack Puccio • Soups & Salads p59 © Kelly Cline • Fish & Seafood p149 © Jack Puccio • Cookies & Candies p165 © Charles Islander • Cakes p185 © Jim Jurica • from bigtsockphoto.com: • Bread & Breakfast p31 © Elzbieta Sekowska • Vegetables & Other Side Dishes p89 © og-vision • from shutterstock.com: • Poultry p133 © Paul Clarke • other: • Beef & Pork p115 © ITStock Free Polka Dot

Contents

Introduction

Mississippi. The Hospitality State. Birthplace of the America's Music. The South's Warmest Welcome. Home. I'm a born-and-raised, been-here-all-my-life Mississippi girl. Kent's father is an Ole Miss graduate that was also born and raised in Mississippi. Kent and his two brothers spent many lazy summer days swimming in Grenada Lake. Though he now resides in the Chattanooga area, much of Kent's family still calls Mississippi home. For both of us, Mississippi is not simply a place, it's our heritage.

And Mississippi's heritage is strong. The Magnolia State has served as home and inspiration to many famous authors, William Faulkner, Eudora Welty, and Willie Morris to name just a few. Mississippi, Birthplace of America's Music, is where the blues, rock n' roll, and country music were born. From blues legend B. B. King, to Elvis Presley The King of Rock n' Roll, to Jimmie Rodgers the Father of Country Music, great music is an important part of Mississippi's history.

Today's Mississippi offers diverse fun for everyone. There are outdoor adventures galore—hunting, fishing, horseback riding, golf, canoeing, bird watching, and more—in the unspoiled natural landscapes of the state. From museums to beaches, casinos to camping, baseball and football to motorcycle and car shows, there is great fun for every member of the family.

Another important part of our heritage is family and where there's family in Mississippi, there is always great food. Any gathering is excuse enough to share food made from recipes handed down through generations of excellent family cooks. From spicy favorites like *Nippy Deviled Eggs, Cajun Catfish, Crawfish Etouffee,* and *Zesty Lima Beans...* to classic southern cooking... *Fried Corn, Mama's Southern-Style Chicken 'n Dumplings, Creamy Banana Pudding,* or *Tomato Gravy...* to all-new down-home favorites like *"Less Fat" Fried Baked Chicken, Southern Soul Bean Salad, Sweet Potato Candy,* and *Easy Coconut Cake...* Not to mention *Biloxi Shrimp Cheese Grits, Homemade Chicken Salad, Divinity,* and *Muscadine Cobbler.*

Mississippi music, cooking, and southern hospitality all come together during the many festivals that are held throughout the state each year. And throughout this book, you'll enjoy information about fun, food-related festivals plus a complete listing of all Mississippi festivals in the back of the book. From **Dudies Burger Festival** in Tupelo to the **Biloxi Seafood Festival**, from **Belzoni's World Catfish Festival** to **Mississippi Pecan Festival** in Richton, from Holly Springs' **Strawberry Plains Festival** to **Vardaman Sweet Potato Festival**, to **Mize Watermelon Festival**, there is a celebration to suit every taste.

This fifth volume in our State Hometown Cookbook Series would not be possible without the generous support of many people. Kent and I spoke to friends, family and many more people throughout the state who generously shared their recipes, their stories, and their memories. Thank you to everyone associated with the food festivals and the Chambers of Commerce and the tourist bureaus who were ever patient and helpful.

Our sincere gratitude goes to Brooke Craig, Anita Musgrove, and Krista Griffin who are forever working tirelessly behind the scenes, and to the rest of the Great American Team: Christy Campbell, Christy Jenkins, Courtney Rust, Kathryn Lang, Mikaela Patrick, Sheena Steadham, and Serena Neal. A very special thank you goes to Lacy Fikes, without you this book may have never made it to the printer, and to Corena Gill, former Mississippi girl. As forever and always, a big thank you goes to our families for their unwavering support; Ally and Macee; Roger, Ryan, and Nicholas—we couldn't do it without you.

Mississippi Hometown Cookbook is for Mississippi residents, visitors, transplanted natives or anyone who wants to experience the unique flavor of our state's special food heritage. We hope you will enjoy this outstanding collection of down-home southern recipes from hometown cooks across the state.

Wishing you many happy kitchen memories,

Sheila Simmons & Kent Whitaker

"And we know that in all things God works for the good of those who love him, who have been called according to his purpose."

Romans 8:28 (NIV)

Appetizers

Shrimp Dip page 16

Blueberry Smoothie

2 cups blueberries, fresh or frozen
8 ounces yogurt, any flavor
1 banana, peeled
1 cup milk, more if desired
1 tablespoon wheat germ, if desired

Blend until smooth and serve.

Gulf South Blueberry Growers
John Braswell, MSU–ES, Poplarville

Chef Jenard Wells Mango Salsa

1 ripe mango, peeled, pitted, and diced (about 1½ cups)
½ medium red onion, finely chopped
1 jalapeño chile, minced (include ribs and seeds for a hotter taste, if desired)
1 small cucumber, peeled and diced (about 1 cup)
3 tablespoons chopped fresh cilantro leaves
3 tablespoons fresh lime juice
Salt and pepper to taste

Also good with diced red bell pepper and jicama.

Combine all ingredients in a bowl. Season to taste with salt and pepper. If the salsa ends up being a little too hot or acidic for your taste, you can temper it by adding some diced avocado.

Chef Jenard Wells,
originally from Michigan City, Mississippi

Yummy Easy Fruit Dip

1 (8-ounce) package cream cheese,
  softened
1 (16-ounce) jar marshmallow cream
Apples
Grapes
Strawberries
Bananas
Any fruit you desire

Beat cream cheese and marshmallow cream until smooth; chill. Serve with fruit for dipping.

Sara Albritton, Canton

Mize Watermelon Festival
July • Mize

It's a time to eat all the watermelon you can handle at the annual Mississippi Watermelon Festival. You'll enjoy seed spitting and watermelon eating contests, live music and more. Since 1978, it's been two days of family fun and entertainment you don't want to miss. If you are a regular, we'll see you there; if you've never been, well, there's plenty of shade and fun for the entire family. Bring your lawn chairs, sit a spell, sample some delicious, ripe, world famous Smith County melons and enjoy some down home southern hospitality. Y'all come see us!

601.733.5647 • mswatermelonfestival.com

Sausage & Cream Cheese Rotel

1 pound sausage, hot or mild
4 (8-ounce) packages cream cheese
2 cups shredded sharp Cheddar cheese
2 cans Rotel tomatoes, hot or mild

Brown sausage; drain. Add to crockpot with cream cheese, Cheddar cheese and Rotel; mix. Cook, stirring occasionally, until melted and hot. Serve hot with tortilla chips. Mmmmm good.

Krista Griffin, Carthage

April's Meaty Crowd-Pleaser Dip

1 (8-ounce) carton whipped cream cheese spread
1 can deviled ham (or substitute corned beef)
2 stalks green onion, chopped
1 teaspoon Worcestershire sauce (if you don't have any, a dash of soy sauce makes a good substitute)
½ teaspoon mustard
A few shakes salt/pepper
A few shakes Soul Seasoning (or other SeasonAll)

This is a party favorite amongst my friends. In fact, if I do not make it, I get racked with guilt from their overwhelming disappointment.

Mix everything well and serve with wheat crackers, rod pretzels, or other goodies of your choosing. Can be doubled.

April Perea, Tupelo

BLT Dip

1 (8-ounce) package cream cheese, softened
¾ cup shredded Romaine lettuce
2 plum tomatoes, seeded and chopped
4 slices bacon, cooked crisp, drained and crumbled

Spread cream cheese on a 9-inch pie plate. Top with lettuce and tomatoes; sprinkle with bacon. Serve with snack crackers or vegetables.

Leanne Townsend, Lena

Cheesy Ranch Chicken Dip

1 (12-ounce) can chicken
1½ tablespoons real bacon bits
3 tablespoons sour cream
1 teaspoon mayonnaise
¼ cup shredded cheese
½ envelope ranch seasoning

Mix well and serve with crackers.

Krista Griffin, Carthage

Spinach and Artichoke Dip with Catfish

3 U.S. Farm Raised Catfish Fillets, baked and flaked
1 (8.5-ounce) can artichokes, drained
1 (16-ounce) bag frozen chopped spinach, defrosted and drained
¾ cup Parmesan cheese, grated (divided)
½ cup diced green onions
1 cup mayonnaise
2 tablespoons chopped fresh garlic
1 teaspoon hot sauce
Salt and pepper to taste

Preheat oven to 350°. Squeeze excess moisture out of artichokes and spinach. Add fish, ½ cup cheese and all remaining ingredients; mix well Transfer to a glass baking dish; sprinkle with remaining ¼ cup cheese. Bake 40 minutes or until hot in the middle and golden brown. Serve warm with your favorite crackers.

The Catfish Institute, Jackson

World Catfish Festival
First Saturday in April • Belzoni

The Annual World Catfish Festival is held the first Saturday in April each year in Beautiful Downtown Belzoni. Great live entertainment, Crowning of Miss Catfish and Little Miss Catfish, Catfish Eating Contest, over 100 arts and crafts vendors, and great activities for the kids. FUN FOR THE ENTIRE FAMILY.

662.247.4838 • worldcatfishfestival.org

Mushroom Dip

4 tablespoons butter
1 garlic clove, minced
1 pound mushrooms, sliced
2 tablespoons chopped parsley
½ teaspoon salt
¼ teaspoon pepper
1 cup sour cream

Melt butter in pan; add garlic, mushrooms, parsley, salt and pepper. Cook until mushrooms are tender; remove from heat. Stir in sour cream. Serve with toast.

Angelia Johnson, Morton

Catfish Dip

4 catfish fillets,
    cooked and flaked
¾ cup sour cream
½ cup picanté sauce
1 package dry Good Seasons Italian Dressing
2 tablespoons lemon juice

Mix well and chill.

World Catfish Festival, Belzoni

Shrimp Dip

1 can cream of shrimp soup
1 (8-ounce) can shrimp, chopped and drained
  (or fresh boiled shrimp, chopped)
1 (8-ounce) package cream cheese, softened
¼ cup finely chopped bell pepper
2 tablespoons finely chopped onion
Dash hot pepper sauce
1 tablespoon chopped fresh or dried parsley

Blend all; refrigerate until ready to serve with crackers.

Note: If you do not have shrimp, substitute 8 ounces finely chopped celery.

Rita S. Franklin, Hattiesburg

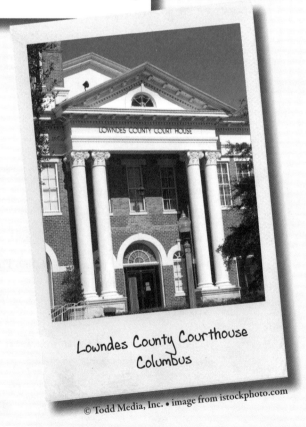

Lowndes County Courthouse
Columbus

© Todd Media, Inc. • image from istockphoto.com

Valerie's Favorite Shrimp Dip

1 pound Mississippi Gulf Shrimp
  (boiled, peeled and chopped)
1 (8-ounce) package Philadelphia cream cheese, softened
1 cup sour cream
1 teaspoon fresh chopped garlic
2 teaspoons Worcestershire sauce
Juice from ½ lemon
½ teaspoon cayenne pepper
1 (8-ounce) can artichoke hearts
2 tablespoons chopped green onions
Sea salt to taste
Sun-dried tomatoes for garnish

I used this recipe to get my daughter to try shrimp for the first time! We took the Biloxi Shrimping Trip offered by Living Marine Adventure Cruise and Valerie saw the catch of the day included dozens of live shrimp and blue crabs. She was amazed that people ate shrimp. That was 2 years ago and she still asks for this recipe whenever Spring Break comes around. You may need to reduce the cayenne pepper for your little one, but Valerie likes it spicy!

Rinse shrimp; set aside to dry. Combine cream cheese, sour cream, garlic, Worcestershire sauce, lemon juice, cayenne pepper and artichoke hearts in a food processor until smooth. Remove to a serving bowl. Fold in shrimp. Sprinkle with green onions and sea salt; garnish with 2 pieces sun-dried tomatoes. Serve with bagel chips and/or warmed pita bread cut in triangles.

Maureen & Valerie Wagner, Biloxi

Mississippi Blue Crab Dip

1 (8-ounce) package cream cheese
⅛ cup mayonnaise (fat free will not work)
1 jalapeño, finely chopped
1 tablespoon Worcestershire sauce
1 pound Mississippi blue crabmeat
⅛ cup chopped green onions

In a saucepan, combine first 4 ingredients and warm until cheese completely softens. Stir until blended. Carefully stir in crab and onion. Heat until warm throughout. Serve warm with crackers.

Roxanne Russell,
Mississippi Department of Marine Resources

Crab Festival
July 4th weekend • Bay St. Louis

Our Lady of the Gulf Church in beautiful Bay St. Louis has hosted the Annual 4th of July Crab Fest since 1984. People come from near and far to feast on the best seafood around, listen to great live music, ride the exciting carnival rides, and browse through 100 arts & crafts booths to find that perfect keepsake. Rated the #1 Fest on the Coast by The Marquee and winner of the 2009 Hancock County Tourism Award, Crab Fest is a good time for the whole family!

228.467.6509 • olgchurch.net/crab.htm

© ParkerDeen • Image from istockphoto.com

Clam Loaf Dip

1 round loaf sourdough bread
3 cans minced clams
½ teaspoon clam juice
2 (8-ounce) packages reduced fat cream cheese
(or regular if you prefer), softened
5 drops Louisiana hot sauce
3 teaspoons Worcestershire sauce
½ teaspoon sea salt
1 tablespoon lemon juice
Dash lime juice

Remove top from bread loaf and save. Pull pieces of bread out of the loaf down to the hard crust, saving bread pieces. Combine remaining ingredients in a medium bowl; mix well. Carefully pour into hollowed-out sourdough loaf. Replace top crust and wrap in heavy foil. Bake at 250° for 2 hours. Meanwhile, lightly toast reserved bread pieces. Serve stuffed bread on a plate surrounded by toasted bread pieces plus your favorite raw veggies for dipping.

Maureen Wagner, Biloxi

Shrimp Spread

½ pound shrimp,
  deveined and cooked
1 (4-ounce) package cream cheese, softened
1 teaspoon grated onion
½ teaspoon lemon juice
½ teaspoon Worcestershire sauce
1 tablespoon heavy cream
½ cup mayonnaise
Salt and pepper to taste

Crumble shrimp with fingers or mash with fork; set aside. Combine cream cheese, onion, lemon juice, Worcestershire and cream. Add shrimp, mayonnaise, salt and pepper. Prepare several hours before serving; refrigerate. Serve on crackers or assorted breads.

Mary McCuen

Pickled Black-Eyed Peas

2 (16-ounce) cans black-eyed peas,
  rinsed and drained
⅔ cup vegetable oil
¾ cup white wine vinegar
1 small onion, diced or thinly sliced
1 garlic clove, minced
½ teaspoon salt
⅛ teaspoon pepper

Stir together all ingredients; cover and chill at least 2 hours. Delicious as a dip with tortilla chips or as a side dish with cold roast beef and potato salad.

Donna Monroe, Greenville

Granny's Bacon Hot Cheese Straws

1 stick butter, softened (more if using pre-shredded cheese)
4 cups freshly shredded Cheddar cheese
2 cups self-rising flour
1 teaspoon salt
1 tablespoon hot sauce
⅔ cup small bacon pieces, cooked
¼ teaspoon ground red pepper

Combine all ingredients in a bowl; set aside to rise for a few minutes. Place on a lightly floured surface. Break into balls and roll into thin straws. Bake at 350° on cookie sheets for 20 to 25 minutes or until golden.

Harriett Whitaker, Grenada

© John Peacock • image from istockphoto.com

Oven-Roasted Salted Pecans

2 pounds (about 5 cups) pecans
5 tablespoons unsalted butter, melted
2 teaspoons kosher salt

Preheat oven to 250°. Spread pecans onto a rimmed baking sheet. Drizzle with butter and salt; toss well. Bake about 1 hour, stirring occasionally, until lightly toasted.

Delma Frazier Rodabough, Amory/McCool

© Charlotte Couchman • image from bigstockphoto.com

Buttered Pecans

3 tablespoons butter
Dash Worcestershire sauce
4 cups pecan halves (not pieces)
2 tablespoons brown sugar

Melt butter in a pan; add Worcestershire sauce. Stir in pecans to fully coat. Sprinkle with brown sugar. Spread on a cookie sheet and bake at 300° until warm. Cool slightly before serving. For a spicy version, add hot sauce to taste (a dash or two).

Harriett Whitaker, Grenada

Gramp's Nuts, Bolts and Screws

2 sticks butter
3 tablespoons Worcestershire sauce
2 tablespoons garlic salt
2 tablespoons onion powder
2 tablespoons celery seasoning
2 teaspoons hot sauce
1 box Wheat Chex cereal
1 box Rice Chex cereal
1 bag pretzel sticks
2 cups Cheerios cereal
1 cup chopped pecans

My grandmother Harriett made this recipe for my grandfather, Gramp (Eli Whitaker Senior). It was her version of the classic holiday mix. It makes a large amount, but can be halved with ease. – Kent

Preheat oven 225°. Melt butter in saucepan. Add Worcestershire sauce, garlic salt, onion powder, celery seasoning and hot sauce. In a large bowl, combine butter sauce with remaining ingredients; stir to mix well. Spread in a single layer on cookie sheets. Bake 1½ hours, turning often with a spoon. Bake until crisp; do not burn. Allow to cool slightly before serving.

Harriett Whitaker, Grenada

Blue Cheese Mushrooms

24 fresh (medium-sized) mushrooms
½ cup chopped green onions
1 tablespoon butter
1 (4-ounce) package blue cheese
½ (8-ounce) package cream cheese

Preheat broiler. Remove stems from mushrooms; reserve caps. Chop stems. Cook chopped stems and onions in butter until soft. Stir in blue cheese and cream cheese; continue to cook until melted and mixed well. Spoon into reserved mushroom caps. Broil 2 to 3 minutes or until brown.

© Brandon Smith • image from istockphoto.com

Deviled Eggs with Kick

8 hard-boiled eggs
¼ cup mayonnaise
1 teaspoon prepared mustard
½ to 1 teaspoon horseradish
¼ teaspoon salt
¼ teaspoon pepper
Paprika

Peel eggs and cut in half lengthwise. Separate yolks from whites. Mash yolks; stir in mayonnaise, mustard, horseradish, salt and pepper. Fill egg-white halves with mixture and chill. Sprinkle with paprika before serving.

Deviled Ham Finger Sandwiches

1 (8-ounce) package cream cheese, softened
1 can deviled ham
¼ cup real mayonnaise
10 small stuffed green olives, finely chopped
36 slices white bread, crust removed

Combine cream cheese, ham, mayo and olives. Spread each of 18 bread slices with 2 teaspoons mixture. Cover with remaining bread. Cut each sandwich into quarters. Makes 72 finger sandwiches.

Leanne Townsend, Lena

Stuffed French Bread

1 whole French bread loaf
1 (8-ounce) package deli-cut ham, chopped
1 (8-ounce) package deli-cut turkey, chopped
1 (8-ounce) package deli-cut roast beef, chopped
2 cups shredded Cheddar cheese
1 cup shredded Swiss cheese
1 (8-ounce) package cream cheese, softened
3 tablespoons butter, melted
1 teaspoon garlic powder
Chives

Cut French bread in half long ways. Hollow out bread on bottom side. Add bread pieces to a bowl with turkey, ham and roast beef. Add Cheddar cheese, swiss cheese, and cream cheese. Mix well. In a separate bowl, combine melted butter and garlic powder. Brush on inside of both sides of French bread (use about ¾ butter mixture leaving enough for top). Stuff hollowed side with meat mixture. Replace top. Brush top with remaining garlic butter. Sprinkle with chives. Wrap in tin foil and bake at 325° for 30 minutes.

Melissa Webb, Ludlow

This is a very versatile dish. It makes a great appetizer dip by removing top and serving with chips, crackers, and top torn into bread pieces for dipping. Or slice into narrow pieces with the top on, and serve as finger sandwiches. Or, slice in bigger pieces as a sandwich to be served with chips as a meal. Anyway you slice it, it will be a hit.

Mississippi Sin

1 loaf French bread
2 (8-ounce) packages cream cheese, softened
1 bundle green onions, chopped
1 (8-ounce) package ham, chopped
2 cups shredded cheese
Worcestershire to taste

Cut a thin slice from top of bread; set aside. Hollow-out bread loaf to ½ inch from edges; reserve bread pieces. Combine remaining ingredients and fill French bread. Cover with reserved top slice; wrap in tin foil. Bake at 350° for 1 hour. Serve with reserved bread cubes, crackers, or potato chips.

Jenny Harrell, Leesburg

Mississippi State Capitol
Jackson

© William Zorn • image from bigstockphoto.com

Sausage Loaf

1 loaf French bread,
   whole not sliced
1 (1-pound) package Jimmy Dean sage sausage
1 (8-ounce) package shredded Cheddar cheese
2 tablespoons milk
1 to 2 tablespoons melted butter
Garlic powder

My mom used to make this all the time. I now make it a lot for get-togethers and everyone always asks for the recipe. It's even good for breakfast with a little syrup.

Slice a very thin "top" layer off of the bread (save it for later) and then hull out the inside of the bread saving half of the bread crumbs from the inside. It will look like a bowl. Brown sausage and drain. In a bowl, combine sausage, cheese and reserved bread crumbs with milk, mixing well. Mash this mixture into the "bread bowl" then place the "top" back on it. Brush top of the bread with melted butter and sprinkle with garlic powder to taste. Bake at 350° about 20 minutes or until top is golden brown. Slice and serve!

D.J. Ludlow

Pimento Cheese

1 (12-ounce) package shredded sharp Cheddar cheese
1 (12-ounce) package shredded mild Cheddar cheese
1 large jar pimentos
1 bunch green onions, chopped
1 cup chopped pecans
3 tablespoons sugar
1 cup (or more) mayonnaise

This recipe belonged to my Mother, Elizabeth Wilson. It is enjoyed a lot in the summer months and can be toasted, too!

Mix all ingredients together and chill. Use more mayonnaise if needed.

Teresa Vanlandingham, Brandon

Pimento Cheese Spread

5 pounds mild Cheddar cheese, grated
1 (28-ounce) can diced pimentos, undrained
1½ quarts Dukes mayonnaise
5 ounces Worcestershire sauce
2 tablespoons ground black pepper
2½ tablespoons Tony Chachere's Original Seasoning
½ teaspoon granulated garlic
2 tablespoons ground sweet basil
2 tablespoons paprika
2 tablespoons chopped basil leaves
1 tablespoon Tabasco
½ teaspoon cayenne pepper

Combine cheese, pimentos, and mayonnaise in small batches and beat with stand mixer until smooth and cheese is broken into smaller pieces. Add remaining ingredients and blend very well. Spoon into airtight containers; refrigerate approximately 24 hours to allow seasonings to blend. Makes about 6½ pounds of spread for a minimum of 100 sandwiches.

Rita S. Franklin, Hattiesburg

Cheese Ball

3 (8-ounce) packages cream cheese, softened
2 bunches green onions, chopped
1 tablespoon Worcestershire sauce
1 tablespoon Accent (no substitutions)
¼ tablespoon garlic salt
3 tablespoons mayonnaise
3 packages wafer thin ham or beef, finely chopped

Cream all together and shape into 1 large or 2 small balls. Keep refrigerated until ready to serve.

Stacy Jones, Louise

Pineapple Cheese Ball

2 (8-ounce) packages cream cheese
1 (8½-ounce) can crushed pineapple, drained
1½ to 2 cups chopped toasted pecans
   (400° oven for 5 minutes), divided
¼ cup finely chopped green bell pepper
2 tablespoons finely chopped onion
1 tablespoon seasoned salt

In medium bowl, mix cheese with fork until soft and smooth. Stir in pineapple and 1 cup Pecans. Add green bell pepper, onion and salt. Shape into a ball. Roll in remaining pecans. Wrap and refrigerate over night. Serve with Ritz crackers.

Donna Monroe, Greenville

Bread & Breakfast

Carol's Crescent Rolls page 39

Hot Hushpuppies

1½ cups yellow cornmeal
½ cup all-purpose flour
1 tablespoon baking powder
1 tablespoon salt
⅔ cup milk
1 egg, beaten
½ cup finely chopped onion
2 tablespoons minced jalapeño pepper

Mix all ingredients together in a bowl. Chill about 30 minutes. Spoon balls of dough into hot oil and fry until golden.

Alan Wilson, Mississippi Gulf Coast

St. Ann's Catfish Festival
May • Lizana

This festival is FUN for the entire family—games, silent auction, live auction, prize bingo (during the day Saturday and Sunday), carnival rides, and of course, FABULOUS FOOD....ESPECIALLY CATFISH, and more! Live entertainment performs throughout the festival. This festival is NOT to be missed—one of the best on the Gulf Coast.

228.832.2560 • catholic-church.org/stann/fish.htm

Hushpuppies

½ cup flour
2 teaspoons baking powder
1 tablespoon sugar
½ teaspoon salt
2 cups cornmeal
1 small onion, finely chopped
1 egg, beaten
¾ cup milk

Sift together dry ingredients. Add onion, egg and milk; stir lightly. Drop by tablespoon into hot deep fat, frying only a few at a time until golden brown. Drain on paper towels.

World Catfish Festival, Belzoni

Mississippi Gulf Oyster Fritters

2 cups fresh Mississippi Gulf Oysters,
    drained and chopped
1 cup flour
½ teaspoon pepper
½ teaspoon chopped parsley
½ teaspoon baking powder
1 onion, minced
2 eggs, beaten

Combine flour, pepper, parsley and baking powder. Add chopped oysters and onion; mix well. Add eggs; mix well. Drop by teaspoons into hot oil and fry until golden brown. If mixture appears to be too thin, add additional flour as needed.

Corn and Freshwater Prawn Fritters

1 cup (16- to 21-count) prawns,
    peeled and deveined (uncooked)
½ cup flour
1 teaspoon salt
¼ teaspoon cayenne
¼ teaspoon black pepper
1½ teaspoons baking powder
1 tablespoon minced garlic
1 egg, separated
1 cup fresh yellow corn kernels
¼ cup minced green onion
1 tablespoon chopped fresh basil
Oil for cooking

Dolores & Steve Fratesi own Lauren Farms Freshwater Prawns in Leland, Mississippi, and offer this fantastic recipe for everyone to enjoy.

Cut prawns into ¼-inch pieces; set aside. In a mixing bowl, combine flour, salt, cayenne, black pepper and baking powder with a fork or whisk. Add garlic; blend again. Whip egg white until stiff but still wet; set aside. Combine egg yolk, prawns, corn, green onions and basil. (Do not over-mix as this will bruise corn kernels and make batter too wet.) Stir in flour mixture with a rubber spatula. Fold in the whipped egg white. Use 2 tablespoons as tools to form 1-inch fritters, and drop in heated oil. Cook evenly (approximately 2 to 3 minutes). You can test with a wooden skewer inserted into the center to make sure batter is cooked through. These fritters are good plain, or you can serve with a rémoulade or jalapeño tartar sauce. Makes 4 servings (approximately 1 dozen fritters).

Dolores & Steve Fratesi,
Lauren Farms, Leland

© Sarah Bossert • image from istockphoto.com

JoAnn's Cornbread Dressing

Cecile's Southern Cornbread:

¼ cup shortening or vegetable oil

2 cups self-rising cornmeal

1½ cups buttermilk (or white milk with ½ teaspoon vinegar)

1 egg

Melt shortening or heat oil in an iron skillet in 425° oven. Meanwhile, mix remaining ingredients. Pour melted shortening in batter; stir. Cook in skillet approximately 25 minutes. Set aside.

JoAnn's Cornbread Dressing:

1 to 2 chicken breasts, bone-in with skin

1 tablespoon salt

¼ teaspoon pepper

½ stick butter

1 pan Cecile's Southern Cornbread, crumbled in food processor

4 slices bread, crumbled in food processor

1 stalk celery, finely chopped

1 small onion, finely chopped

1 teaspoon sage

2 teaspoons parsley flakes

2 eggs, beaten

This is my Mother-in-law's recipe. She makes this during the holidays, and I've been asking for it for years. The only problem, it had never been written down. So in order to get it, I made it with her and wrote it down as we went.

Boil chicken in water to cover with salt, pepper and butter until done (approximately 20 to 25 minutes). Save 4 cups broth for the dressing. Cool chicken then cut in small bite-size pieces. Combine, chicken, cornbread, bread, celery, onion, sage, parsley and reserved broth. Mix well. Check flavor, and add more seasoning if desired. Add eggs. Mix very well; you can use a potato masher to break up the clumps. Bake in a 2-quart casserole approximately 30 minutes at 350°.

Cecil & Randy Dunn, Hattiesburg

Nina's Cornbread Dressing

1 cup chopped onion
1 cup chopped celery
Olive oil (or butter)
1 pan/skillet cooked cornbread, crumbled
4 pieces white bread, torn into small pieces
4 cans chicken broth
1 can cream of chicken soup
4 boiled eggs, chopped
Salt and pepper

Sauté onions and celery in olive oil (or butter). Spray 9x13-inch baking pan with Pam. Mix cornbread and white bread in pan. Add chicken broth, soup, onions, celery and eggs. Salt and pepper to taste. Mix well. Bake at 350° until brown, about 45 minutes to 1 hour.

Phil Hardwick, Jackson

My mother made this recipe at Thanksgiving for several decades. Eventually, children and grandchildren were assigned dishes to bring for the family Thanksgiving meal. I was designated the cornbread dressing preparer. My mother gave me this recipe, and the next Thanksgiving's cornbread dressing was a hit. So much so that I have made it many times for other communal meal occasions. Nowadays, during the fall and winter season when there is a community meal of any kind I often hear, "And Phil, would you bring your cornbread dressing?" By the way, there is never any left to take back home. Thanks Mother!

© Michael Phillips • image from istockphoto.com

Executive Cornbread Dressing

10 cups crumbled cornbread
8 cups toasted white-bread pieces
3 cups chicken or turkey broth
3 cups diced yellow onion
2⅔ cups diced celery
2 green bell peppers, diced
2½ sticks butter, divided (melt all but 4 tablespoons)
⅔ cup chopped parsley
1 teaspoon dry sage, rubbed (or 2 teaspoons fresh)
1 teaspoon dry thyme (or 2 teaspoons fresh)
4 eggs, beaten
4 hard-cooked eggs, chopped (optional)
2 pints raw oysters (optional)
1 pound smoked sausage, diced, cooked, and drained (optional)

Preheat oven to 350° convection or 400° conventional. Soak cornbread and bread in broth. Cook onions, celery and peppers in 4 tablespoons butter until tender. Combine everything and place in greased pan. Bake 1 hour or until desired doneness. Serves 24.

Chef Matt Huffman,
Executive Chef for the Governor of Mississippi.

Fried Hot Water Cornbread

2 cups self-rising white or yellow cornmeal
2 tablespoons flour
1 egg, beaten
1 tablespoon sugar
1½ cups hot water
Vegetable oil for frying

Combine cornmeal, flour, egg, sugar and hot water in large bowl. Heat vegetable oil in skillet until hot; reduce heat to medium. Place 1 heaping tablespoon cornmeal mixture for each bread patty in skillet. Fry 3 to 5 minutes or until golden brown; flip and repeat for other side. Cool on paper towels.

Harriett Whitaker, Grenada

Mexican Cornbread

2 eggs, slightly beaten
1 cup buttermilk
¼ cup oil
1 cup cream-style corn
1½ cups self-rising cornmeal
1 teaspoon salt
2 tablespoons chopped green bell peppers
2 hot peppers, chopped
1 cup grated cheese, divided

Mix all ingredients together, except cheese. Pour half into hot, greased 9x12-inch pan. Sprinkle with ½ cup cheese. Add remaining mixture and top with remaining cheese. Bake 25 minutes at 450°.

Delma Frazier Rodabough, Amory/McCool

Granny's Sweet Cornmeal Muffins

¾ cup cornmeal
1¼ cups flour
½ teaspoon salt
4 teaspoons baking powder
2 tablespoons sugar
2 tablespoons shortening, melted
1 cup milk
1 egg, beaten
¼ teaspoon ground red pepper

Sift dry ingredients together in a bowl. Add remaining ingredients, and beat well. Bake in greased muffin tin at 350° about 20 minutes.

Harriett Whitaker, Grenada

Carol's Crescent Rolls

½ cup warm water (**105 to 115°**)
1 package active dry yeast
½ cup milk
½ cup butter
⅓ cup sugar
¾ teaspoon salt
1 egg, beaten
4 cups (approximately) sifted flour, divided

The whole family gobbles these up each Thanksgiving. Make plenty!

Use candy thermometer to get water to right temperature. Sprinkle yeast over warm water; let stand 5 minutes. Stir to dissolve. Scald milk by cooking over medium heat until "skin" appears on bottom of pan. While milk is scalding, slice butter very thinly into a large bowl. Add sugar and salt. Add hot milk; cool to lukewarm. Add yeast, egg, and 2 cups flour. Beat well. Add just enough additional flour to make a dough that does not stick to bowl. Beat well. Turn out onto floured board and knead lightly. Put in large bowl treated with nonstick spray. Turn to coat on all sides. Cover and let rise until doubled (about 1 hour). Divide dough in half. Roll each half out to form a 12-inch circle. Cut each circle into 12 pie shaped pieces. Roll up from wide end and place on greased baking sheet, pointed end down. Let rise until doubled (about 30 minutes). Bake at 400° for 15 minutes. Cool on rack. If you are going to freeze and reheat them, bake only about 10 to 12 minutes.

*L. Randall 'Randy' Finfrock
and his sister Carol Virginia Toombs, Meridian*

Cha-Cha's Yeast Rolls

½ cup shortening
2 cups milk
1 rounded teaspoon salt
½ cup sugar
2 packages yeast
¼ cup cool water
5 rounded cups flour, divided
1 teaspoon baking powder
½ teaspoon baking soda
Butter

My grandmother made the best yeast rolls. We called her Cha-Cha, and I treasure memories of cutting out the dough with her in her kitchen for special dinners such as Easter and Christmas.

Heat shortening, milk, salt and sugar until it melts. Pour in stainless steel bowl; cool to very warm, but not hot. About 110° to 115°. Add yeast to cool water; let it soften. Stir into very warm milk mixture. Add 3 cups flour and stir well. Put cloth over top and let rise until double (about 2 hours). Work down with spoon or hands. Add remaining 2 cups flour (give or take ½ cup), baking powder and baking soda; mix well. Cover tightly; will keep in refrigerator for 7 days. Roll out dough as needed, cut in rounds, fold in half, top with melted butter. Allow to rise until doubled in size. Bake at 375° until brown.

Fran Stallings Peacock, Jackson

Water Tower
Poplarville

© Blueberry Jubilee

Fran's Favorite Cinnamon Rolls

1 recipe Cha-Cha's Yeast Rolls (opposite page)
½ stick butter plus 1 tablespoon butter, divided
2 tablespoons sugar
2 tablespoons ground cinnamon
½ to ¾ cup chopped pecans, optional
2 tablespoons milk
1 teaspoon vanilla
1 to 2 cups powdered sugar, depending on your taste of consistency

Snow is very uncommon here in Mississippi, but when it does snow, there is nothing better than one of these cinnamon rolls with a hot cup of coffee.

Preheat oven to 375°. Melt ½ stick butter. In a separate bowl, combine sugar and cinnamon. Roll out half of dough to almost ¼- to ⅛-inch thick. Make a rough rectangle. Pour ½ melted butter on dough and smooth all over. Sprinkle ½ cinnamon and sugar mixture over butter. If desired, sprinkle ½ nuts over cinnamon and sugar. Roll up dough lengthwise and seal edge with water. Cut into 1- to 1½-inch thick slices. Place rolls flat on ungreased cookie sheet, about 1 to 2 inches apart. Repeat with remainder of dough, butter, cinnamon/sugar mixture and nuts. Allow to rise until doubled (about 1 hour). Bake 10 to 15 minutes, or until brown. Cool. To prepare Icing, melt remaining 1 tablespoon butter in a deep microwave safe bowl (I use a 2-cup measuring cup). Stir in milk and vanilla. Stir in powdered sugar, a little at a time, until desired consistency is achieved. Less powdered sugar makes a thinner glaze; more powdered sugar, makes a thicker icing. Makes about 2 dozen.

Fran Stallings Peacock, Jackson

Carol's Hot Cross Buns

¾ cup milk
½ cup Crisco
⅓ cup sugar
1 teaspoon salt
¼ cup warm water
1½ packages active dry yeast
1 egg, beaten
¾ cup currants
½ teaspoon mace
3¼ cups flour
Canola oil
1 egg white, beaten
1 cup powdered sugar
2 tablespoons hot water
½ teaspoon vanilla

My sister Carol makes this bread and it is wonderful for Easter breakfast or lunch.

Cook milk over medium heat to scald (until leaves a "skin" on bottom of pan). In large bowl, combine Crisco, sugar and salt. Add hot milk; stir. Cool to lukewarm. Pour water into small bowl; add yeast. Let rest 5 minutes, then stir to dissolve. Add yeast mixture, 1 beaten whole egg, currants, mace and flour to milk mixture. Blend well. Place in greased bowl, turning to coat on all sides. Cover with towel and let rise about 2 hours. Turn out onto floured board. Knead 1 minute. Form into 18 2-inch balls. Arrange in 2 8x8-inch greased baking pans (about 1-inch apart). Snip a cross in each ball using greased shears. Brush tops with egg white. Cover with towel and let rise until doubled (about 1 hour). Heat oven to 350°. Bake 25 minutes or until done. Cool on wire rack. Fill cross with glaze made of powdered sugar, water and vanilla.

*L. Randall 'Randy' Finfrock
and his sister Carol Virginia Toombs, Meridian*

Pull-Apart Cheesy Onion Buns

Frozen yeast rolls,
    thawed and risen per directions (3 to 5 hours)
½ pound cheese cubes
1 stick butter, melted
1 envelope dry onion soup mix

After they have risen, slice yeast rolls in half. Wrap each roll around 1 cheese cube, sealing completely. Melt butter in shallow pan. Stir in dry onion soup. Roll dough balls in butter mixture. Place in treated bundt pan. Bake at 350° about 25 minutes (will be very brown on top). Cool, then pull apart to eat with your meal.

Krista Griffin, Carthage

Best Nut Loaf

¾ cup sugar
3 cups sifted all-purpose flour
3½ teaspoons baking powder
1½ teaspoons salt
1 egg, beaten
1½ cups milk
2 tablespoons oil
¾ cup broken walnuts

Preheat oven 350°. Sift dry ingredients together. In a separate bowl, combine egg, milk and oil; add to dry ingredients, mixing well. Stir in nuts. Turn into greased 9½x5x3-inch loaf pan. Bake about 1 hour or until done. Remove from pan; cool.

Alice Henderson, Florence

Pecan Pie Muffins

1 cup light brown sugar
½ cup all-purpose flour
2 eggs
⅔ cup melted butter
1 cup chopped pecans

Preheat oven to 350º. Mix all ingredients in a bowl with a wooden spoon. Pour into a greased mini muffin pan, filling each cup ⅔ full. Bake 12 to 15 minutes. Makes 2½ to 3 dozen.

Delma Frazier Rodabough,
Amory /McCool

Blueberry Butter

½ cup butter
2 tablespoons honey
¼ teaspoon cinnamon
Dash orange zest
¼ teaspoon allspice
¼ cup blueberries
¼ teaspoon nutmeg

Blend in blender and store in refrigerator. Serve on hot biscuits, homemade bread, toast and more.

Gulf South Blueberry Growers,
Blue Tara Organic Blueberry Farm, Poplarville

Sugar 'n' Spice Blueberry Muffins

1 package bran muffin mix
   plus ingredients to prepare per package directions
1 cup fresh or frozen blueberries,
   rinsed and drained
½ teaspoon ground allspice
¼ cup butter or margarine
¼ cup sugar
1 teaspoon ground cinnamon

Prepare mix according to package directions. Gently fold in blueberries and allspice. Spoon into greased muffin pan. Bake as directed on package. While muffins, cook melt butter. In a separate bowl, combine sugar and cinnamon. Remove muffins from pan and, while hot, dip tops into melted butter and then into sugar mixture. Serve warm.

Gulf South Blueberry Growers
Ambers Blueberry Farm, Waynesboro

The Blueberry Jubilee
Second Saturday in June • Poplarville

The Blueberry Jubilee was originally born as an arts & crafts festival in 1984. It's the first and only festival in Poplarville. You can expect to enjoy live music, arts & crafts, food, car show, the 5k run, the pie eating contest, and of course the Blueberry Recipe Contest. This is an event you will not want to miss. It's family fun for all ages.

601.759.8377 • blueberryjubilee.org

Carol's Pumpkin Bread

3½ cups sifted flour
2 teaspoons soda
1½ teaspoons salt
1 teaspoon cinnamon
1 teaspoon nutmeg
1 teaspoon allspice
3 cups sugar
1 cup canola oil
4 eggs
⅔ cup water
2 cups canned pumpkin
1½ cups chopped pecans
1 cup raisins, optional

This is my sister's Pumpkin Bread recipe. It's good for breakfast, or as a snack on a hayride! Carol loves making fun items for the holidays.

Mix flour, soda, salt, cinnamon, nutmeg, allspice and sugar in a large bowl. In a separate bowl, combine remaining ingredients. Make a well in the center of dry ingredients, and add liquid ingredients. Blend well to make batter. Pour into 3 well-greased and floured loaf pans. Bake at 350° for 1 hour. Cool slightly in the pan (about 10 minutes). Turn out onto a wire rack to cool. Cool completely before cutting or covering and storing.

L. Randall 'Randy' Finfrock and his sister
Carol Virginia Toombs, Meridian

© Darren Fisher • image from bigstockphoto.com

Apple Bread

2 (¼-ounce) packages active dry yeast
1 tablespoon sugar
1 cup warm water
½ cup apple sauce
1 cup low fat vanilla yogurt
¼ cup butter, melted
2 tablespoons honey
1½ tablespoons salt
3½ cups whole wheat flour
2 cups all-purpose flour
1 egg, beaten
1 teaspoon water

Dissolve yeast and sugar in warm water; allow to rest 5 minutes. Stir in apple sauce, yogurt, butter, honey and salt. Add flour, a little at a time, and beat as you go, until dough becomes stiff. Turn out on floured counter and knead until dough is smooth. Place dough back in bowl and cover with a damp towel; allow to rise until doubled. Punch dough down to remove air; divide in half and place in 2 greased loaf pans. Cover and rise until doubled. Heat oven to 425º. Beat egg with 1 teaspoon water. Brush loaves with egg wash. Bake 10 minutes. Reduce oven temperature to 375º; bake about 25 minutes or until golden brown on top.

Easy Banana Bread

3 ounces cream cheese
3 eggs
3 ripe bananas, mashed
1 box yellow cake mix

Preheat oven to 350º. Beat cream cheese and eggs. Add bananas; mix well. Add cake mix; mix well. Pour into treated loaf pan. Bake 1 hour. Cool in pan 10 minutes then remove. Enjoy.

Anita Musgrove, Brandon

Southern Pecan Beer Bread

2¼ cups all-purpose flour
3 tablespoons sugar
1 tablespoon baking powder
½ teaspoon baking soda
¼ teaspoon salt
12 ounces Southern Pecan Nut Brown Ale
2 tablespoons olive oil
½ cup chopped pecans, optional

Preheat oven to 400°. Spray 8-inch loaf pan with nonstick cooking spray. Combine flour, sugar, baking powder, baking soda and salt in a large bowl. Make a well in the center. Pour in beer and olive oil (add pecans, if desired); mix until just blended. It may be a bit lumpy. Pour batter into prepared loaf pan and bake 45 minutes until golden brown.

Lazy Magnolia Brewing Co., Lee Hood, Kiln

Gingerbread

1 cup shortening
1½ cups brown sugar
2 eggs
1 cup molasses
1 teaspoon baking soda
1 cup hot water
3½ cups flour
1 tablespoon ginger
2 teaspoons cinnamon
2 teaspoons nutmeg

Cream shortening. Add sugar and cream again. Add eggs; beat well. Stir in molasses. Dissolve baking soda in hot water. Add dry ingredients alternately with hot water to creamed mixture. Bake at 350° in treated 9x13-inch pan about 50 minutes or until top springs back when pressed lightly. Remove from pan. Cool; cut in squares and serve with whipped cream.

Bread Pudding with Whiskey Sauce

Bread Pudding

2 loaves Pepperidge Farm Cinnamon Bread
   or Cinnamon Raisin Bread
7 large eggs
2 cups milk
2 cups whipping cream
2 cups sugar

Crumble bread into baking dish. Whisk together eggs, milk and whipping cream; whisk in sugar. Pour over bread. Let stand 30 minutes. Bake at 350º for 35 to 40 minutes. Delicious served with Whiskey Sauce on top.

Whiskey Sauce

3 cups whipping cream
1½ cups sugar
½ cup Irish cream or whiskey
3 tablespoons cornstarch
3 tablespoons water

© Leo Lintang • image from bigstockphoto.com

Bring whipping cream, sugar and whiskey to a boil in a medium saucepan. In a small bowl, stir together cornstarch and water until smooth. Add to saucepan. Simmer until thickened. Serve over Bread Pudding.

Leanne Townsend, Lena

Sweet Potato Biscuits

2½ cups self-rising flour
1 cup mashed cooked sweet potatoes
2 tablespoons sugar
1 teaspoon salt
¼ cup (½ stick) butter, softened
Milk, as needed

This recipe has quickly become a family favorite. They are great fresh out of the oven, or leftover as a snack.

Combine first five ingredients; add a spoonful of milk at a time until dough is moist. Turn dough onto a floured surface and roll to ½-inch thick. Cut with biscuit cutter and bake at 400° until biscuits are beginning to brown. Serve hot.

The White Family, Oxford

Sausage & Biscuits

1 can biscuits
1 pound sausage, cooked and drained
6 to 8 eggs, beaten
2 cups sharp Cheddar cheese

Split biscuits and place in 9x13-inch pan. Combine sausage, eggs and cheese; pour over biscuits. Bake at 350° for 35 minutes.

Mary Carter, Yazoo City

Fran's Favorite Biscuits

2 cups flour
4 teaspoons baking powder
¼ teaspoon baking soda
1 scant teaspoon salt
1 tablespoon sugar
½ cup lard, frozen
¾ cup buttermilk
1 egg
3 tablespoons melted butter for tops

Biscuits have always been a central part of Mississippi fare. It took me years of keeping a biscuit journal to arrive at this version, and they go well with anything. For a more savory biscuit, add ½ teaspoon Tony Chachere's, or add more sugar for a sweet treat.

Sift together flour, baking powder, baking soda, salt and sugar. Add these dry ingredients to a food processor with the blade attachment. Add frozen lard and combine in processor until lard is fully incorporated and the mixture has a cornmeal consistency. Beat buttermilk and egg in a stand mixer with a whisk attachment at least 2 minutes. Empty flour mixture into a large bowl, make a well in the middle, and pour in the egg and buttermilk mixture. Stir gently, just enough to combine. Return dough to the processor with dough attachment, and allow dough to rest 10 minutes. Preheat oven to 375º. Run food processor with dough attachment just long enough for dough to achieve a singular consistency within the processor, about 35 to 45 seconds. Turn out on a lightly floured surface. Press out with well-floured hands into a rectangle. Fold letter-style, then press down and fold letter-style in the opposite direction. Repeat 4 to 5 times. Finally, press to a ¾-inch thickness and cut in 2-inch square biscuits with a large kitchen knife. Brush tops with melted butter. Bake 12 to 16 minutes.

Fran Stallings Peacock, Jackson

Crystal Springs Tomato Fest
Last Saturday in June • Crystal Springs

For centuries, the tomato was called a "love apple." Nearly three hundred years later, Crystal Springs tomatoes were much in demand. So great was the exultation over "Tomato Days" that a giant Tomato Festival was held, complete with parades, bands, and speeches. Each of the three festivals had a Tomato Queen; but everyone knew, without being told, that the King was a red-faced fellow named Tomato! When you come to Tomatopolis of the World, you can find fine food, live entertainment, a flea market, a farmers market, and whoa, look out, there are people dancing in the street!

601.892.2711 • crystalspringsmiss.com

Tomato Gravy

¼ cup vegetable oil
Salt and pepper
6 tablespoons flour
1 can tomato sauce
1 can water

Heat oil in skillet to hot. Add salt and pepper to taste. Cover with flour; stir well. Add tomato sauce; stir well. Fill can with water and add to skillet; stir well. Simmer until gravy thickens. Serve over hot buttermilk biscuits.

Krista Griffin, Carthage

Bacon Tomato Gravy

6 slices bacon
½ cup chopped onion
4 tablespoons flour
2 cups milk, heated
1 cup chopped tomatoes
Salt and pepper to taste

Cook bacon to crisp; remove to drain. Sauté onions in bacon drippings; remove from pan reserving drippings. Add flour to pan; cook and stir with a fork until dark brown. Add bacon, onions, milk, tomatoes, salt and pepper. Simmer until tomatoes are tender and gravy is thick.

Leanne Townsend, Lena

Grenada Country Sausage Gravy

½ pound mild sausage
3 tablespoons butter
⅓ cup all-purpose flour
5 cups whole milk
1½ teaspoons salt
1½ teaspoons pepper
Dash sugar

This recipe is inspired from my grandmother's gravy. I loved her gravy and her French toast! – Kent

Cook sausage in a skillet until done; drain slightly. Add butter, flour, milk, salt, pepper and a dash of sugar. Simmer over medium-high heat stirring constantly until desired thickness. Add more milk to thin or flour to thicken, if needed.

Wake-UP Breakfast Casserole

1 loaf (approximately) sandwich bread
1 pound sausage, browned and drained
1 (12-ounce) bag shredded Cheddar cheese
1 dozen eggs, beaten well

Press 1 layer of bread in the bottom of a treated casserole dish, ensuring the bottom is completely covered. Cover with sausage then sprinkle with cheese. Pour eggs over top. Bake at 350° until eggs are set, approximately 25 minutes. Enjoy.

Brenda Fiscus, Lena

Meema's Cheese Strata

12 slices bread, without crust
Mustard
1 pound mild Cheddar cheese, grated
1 pound sausage, (browned, drained and crumbled)
Butter, softened
4 eggs, beaten
2½ cups milk
1 teaspoon salt

This is hand-written in my grandmother's own family cookbook. It is out of this world. It's very hearty and great for any time of year. My grandmother loved this recipe, and so do I.

Very lightly coat 6 pieces bread with mustard and place in a greased 9x12-inch pan. Cover with cheese then top with sausage. Very lightly coat remaining 6 pieces bread with butter and place over sausage; cover with cheese. Mix eggs, milk and salt in a bowl and pour over all. Cover and refrigerate at least 1 hour, best overnight. Bake, covered, at 350° for 1 hour.

John Stamoulis, USCG,
in honor of his grandmother, Tina Kennedy, Gulfport

Granny's Mississippi French Toast

4 to 5 large eggs
⅔ cup milk
½ tablespoon cinnamon or more to taste
½ tablespoon brown sugar
1 tablespoon French vanilla coffee creamer
10 to 12 pieces Texas Toast
Butter

Beat eggs. Add milk, cinnamon, brown sugar and creamer; beat well. Soak each piece of bread evenly and pan-fry in a skillet with hot butter until golden and puffed. Sprinkle with more brown sugar, if desired. Serve hot. Baked version: Layer ½ toast in a baking dish, cover with ½ egg mixture. Repeat layers. Chill 1 to 2 hours then bake at 350° about 40 minutes or until golden and puffed. Top with strawberries, blueberries or pecans, if desired.

This recipe started my cooking career. It is the first recipe I remember learning. Every time we visited my grandparents in Grenada, Mississippi, my grandmother and I would make this for breakfast. The only difference between her version and mine is I substitute French vanilla coffee creamer for vanilla flavoring. – Kent

© Joe Michl • image from istockphoto.com

Granny's Waffles

2 cups flour
1 teaspoon salt
4 teaspoons baking powder
3 egg whites
1¾ cups milk
½ cup oil
Dash vanilla

My Granny made great waffles. This recipe uses egg whites, but I found that using 2 whole eggs works well too.

Sift together flour, salt and baking powder. Beat egg whites until light. Stir in milk. Add oil; stir. Mix with dry ingredients and beat well. Cook in greased waffle maker until golden.

Harriett Whitaker, Grenada

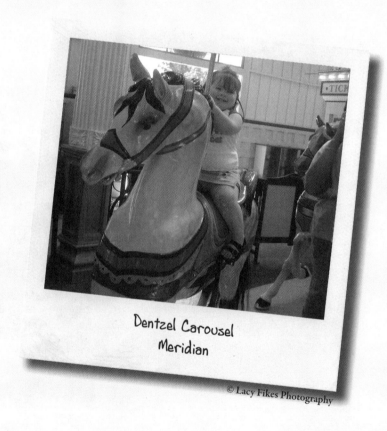

Dentzel Carousel
Meridian

© Lacy Fikes Photography

Momma's Biloxi Breakfast Skillet

½ cup chopped onion
1 cup chopped green bell pepper
½ stick butter
1½ cups chopped cooked ham
3 medium potatoes, (cooked, peeled and cubed)
Salt and pepper to taste
6 eggs, beaten

My mother was raised in Mississippi and this was one of her favorite recipes. She and her mom would make it almost once a week from leftovers from the week's meals. She said it was always different depending on the leftovers. The only thing that was always the same-it was made in her kitchen in Biloxi. This recipe is the one she seemed to settle on over the years and passed on to me. Now it is one of my husband's favorites.

In skillet, cook onion and green bell pepper in butter until tender. Add ham, potatoes, salt and pepper. Cook over medium heat 10 minutes, stirring, until potatoes are brown on the edges. To finish in the skillet, add eggs and cook until eggs are done. For a baked dish, spoon mixture into a casserole dish, pour beaten eggs over top and bake at 350° until eggs are done. Serve hot. Sprinkle with real bacon bits, if desired.

Belinda Johnston & Family, Raised in Biloxi

Grits Soufflé

1½ cups quick grits
6 cups water
2 teaspoons salt
¼ cup butter
1½ cups shredded Cheddar cheese
5 eggs, beaten

Boil grits in salted water according to time on package directions. Stir in butter and cheese until cheese is melted; cool. When cheese grits are lukewarm, add eggs and pour into a greased 2-quart baking dish or soufflé dish. Bake 45 minutes at 350°. Serves 6.

Cheese Grits

1⅓ cups quick grits
   plus ingredients to prepare per package directions
1 pound Velveeta cheese
1 stick butter
½ cup half & half
4 eggs, beaten
Salt and pepper to taste
1 teaspoon cayenne pepper or to taste

I serve these Cheese Grits with fried shrimp or fried catfish. Add coleslaw and hushpuppies, and you have a great Southern meal.

Prepare grits per package directions. Add Velveeta, butter and half & half. Pour small amount of grits into eggs (so as not to "cook" eggs), and then return all to pan, stirring well. Add cayenne pepper. Place in 9x13-inch buttered dish and cover with foil; bake at 375° for 25 minutes. Remove foil and continue to bake 10 minutes. Serve warm.

Pam Simpson, Vancleave

Soups & Salads

Cous'n Betty's Mississippi Seafood Gumbo

¼ cup bacon grease
⅓ cup flour
1 medium onion, chopped
½ medium green bell pepper, chopped
2 stalks celery, chopped
1 pound okra, cut in small pieces
2 cloves garlic, chopped
2 quarts water (approximate)
1 medium can tomatoes
Salt and pepper, to taste
4 pounds shrimp, heads removed and peeled
   (2 pounds makes a good gumbo if larger quantity is not available)
1 pound (meat of about 12 large crabs) crabmeat
   (a smaller amount of canned crabmeat can be used)
Dash Worcestershire sauce, optional
½ to 1 teaspoon vinegar, optional

This gumbo is better the next day if it lasts that long. It freezes well. Sautéing the shrimp and crab briefly in a little bacon grease before putting them in the gumbo will help remove the fishy taste. This recipe was an old family recipe. It was graciously passed on to a new neighbor unfamiliar with coastal living and seafood cooking. It has been a favorite of our family now for almost fifty years.

Optional ingredients (but good!):

Left-over beef gravy, roast, stew meat, etc.
Substitute a cup of gravy for some of the water
Left-over baked ham in chunks

Heat bacon grease in large iron skillet, add flour and stir until nice and brown. Add onions, green bell peppers, celery, okra and garlic; brown well, stirring often. While vegetables are cooking, put water, tomatoes, salt, pepper and optional items in a large pot. Add browned vegetables and cook about 30 minutes. Add cleaned shrimp and crabmeat; simmer for not less than 1 hour (better if cooked 2 or 3 hours). COOK VERY SLOWLY. Vinegar will bring out flavor. It can be added any time as can the Worcestershire sauce. Serve over fluffy steamed rice.

Bettye Lusk Arnold, Hattiesburg

Demaris' Crawfish Bisque Soup

1 stick butter
⅔ cup chopped green onions
1 pound mushrooms, sliced
2 cans cream of potato soup
1 can cream of mushroom soup
2 cans whole-kernel corn, drained
2 pints half & half
1 (8-ounce) package cream cheese
1 pound crawfish tails (shrimp or crabmeat can be substituted)
1 to 2 teaspoons Tony Chachere's Seasoning

This is so good it seems I can never make enough to please the crowd.

Heat butter in medium-sized stockpot over medium heat. Add green onions and mushrooms; sauté until soft. Add both soups; cook until heated through. Add remaining ingredients. Continue to cook, stirring often, until soup reaches desired consistency.

Demaris Lee, Petal

MS Coast Coliseum Crawfish Festival
Mid-April • Biloxi

Mudbugs, Music, Midway Rides, and Contests!! The Crawfish Festival has enjoyed headline entertainers such as Gary Allan, Jason Aldean, Blake Shelton, and many more; plus zydeco and Cajun bands. Then there's the Midway Rides for little tykes and thrill seekers alike. Check out the numerous vendors and Midway Games. Highlighting the event is the Crawfish Cook-off where over 20 teams compete for cash and trophies, and the public can taste the recipes and cast their vote for the People's Choice Champion. It's all there at the MS Coast Coliseum Crawfish Festival in Biloxi.

228.594.3700 • mscoastcoliseum.com

Easy Crab Soup

1 large onion, diced
4 stalks celery, finely chopped
1 stick butter
1 can cream of mushroom soup
1 can cream of celery soup
1 quart half & half
1 pound lump crabmeat
Salt, pepper and Tony Chachere's to taste

This recipe came from a dear church friend. It is so good it rivals any crab soup found in the finest restaurant. Every time I serve it, the compliments just pour in. And it's quick and easy. This is really one of my family's favorite meals. I serve it with a salad and crusty French bread.

Sauté onion and celery in butter until vegetables are soft. Add both soups, half & half and crabmeat. Season to taste. Simmer gently, stirring occasionally, for 1 hour.

Pam Simpson, Vancleave

Mississippi Gulf Oyster Soup

1 quart Mississippi Gulf Oysters
2 to 3 tablespoons flour
1 cup water
2 strips bacon, finely chopped
1 stalk celery, finely chopped
3 green onions, finely chopped
3 to 4 cups whole milk
Salt and pepper to taste

Rinse oysters and set aside. Mix flour with water, mix well, and set aside. Place bacon, celery and onions in heavy saucepan on low heat. Stir often until bacon browns a bit and celery and onions are soft. Add whole milk, keep heat low. Salt and pepper to taste. When milk is good and hot (do not boil), add oysters; cook until oysters curl. Add additional flour for thickness, if desired. Serve with oyster crackers.

Linda McCarthy,
Mississippi Department of Marine Resources

Mississippi Red Snapper Soup

1 pound Mississippi Red Snapper fillets
2 small potatoes
2 small carrots
4 teaspoons olive oil
2 cups boiling water
1 tablespoon white wine vinegar
Salt to taste
2 quarts fish broth or canned chicken broth
¾ cup long grain rice
2 tablespoons minced fresh parsley
¼ teaspoon dried red pepper flakes
Freshly ground black pepper to taste

Cut fish fillets in ½-inch pieces. Peel and dice potatoes. Peel and shred carrots. Heat oil in a large kettle. Add potatoes and sauté over high heat until lightly browned. Add shredded carrots and sauté until slightly softened. Add boiling water along with vinegar and salt. Simmer until vegetables are tender, about 10 minutes. Add broth and rice and simmer 15 minutes. Add fish and simmer until fish is cooked and rice is tender, about 5 minutes longer. Remove kettle from heat and stir in parsley and red pepper flakes. Adjust seasoning as necessary. Ladle into warm bowls and sprinkle with freshly ground black pepper. Serve immediately. Makes 8 to 10 servings.

Irvin Jackson,
Mississippi Department of Marine Resources

"Rags to Riches" Bean Soup

2 cups dried great Northern beans
1 small white onion, diced
2 cloves garlic, pressed
1 ham hock
1 carrot, diced
1 potato, diced
½ teaspoon season-all
1 lemon, juiced
2 tablespoons brown sugar
Salt and pepper to taste
1 can Rotel tomatoes

Soak cleaned beans overnight; drain. Add beans and remaining ingredients, except tomatoes, to a large stockpot and cover with water by 1 inch. Bring to a boil then simmer about 1 hour; stir and add additional water as may be needed. Add tomatoes and simmer another hour. Add a couple dashes dried parsley last few minutes, if desired.

Virginia Hammond

© MSPhotographic • image from bigstockphoto.com

Betty Bouffant's Santa Fe Soup

2 pounds ground beef
1 onion, chopped
2 packets ranch-style dressing mix
2 (1¼-ounce) packets taco seasoning mix
1 (16-ounce) can black beans
1 (16-ounce) can kidney beans
1 (16-ounce) can pinto beans
1 (16-ounce) can Rotel
1 (16-ounce) can tomato wedges
2 cups water

Garnish:

Sour cream
Shredded Cheddar cheese
Green onions, sliced

Brown ground beef and onions in a small stockpot or large saucepan. Add ranch dressing mix and taco seasoning. Add canned ingredients; do not drain. Add water and bring to a boil. Reduce heat to medium and cook, stirring as necessary, for 20 to 30 minutes. Garnish each bowl with sour cream, shredded Cheddar cheese and sliced green onions as desired.

Jimmie Saucier, Ridgeland

Hamburger & Chicken Soup

2 chicken breasts
4 cans chicken broth
2 onions, chopped (divided)
2 pounds hamburger meat
2 bags frozen corn
2 bags frozen butter beans
4 cans Campbell's tomato soup
5 pounds potatoes, peeled and chopped
Noodles, optional
Salt and pepper to taste
Red pepper to taste

In a large soup pot, boil chicken in broth with 1 onion. In a separate pan, brown hamburger meat with remaining onion; drain. Add meat and remaining ingredients to pot. Bring to boil, reduce heat, cover and simmer 1 hour or longer (at least until vegetables are tender).

Kristy Lepard, Good Hope

The Mississippi Governor's Mansion
Jackson

© Hope Evans • image from bigstockphoto.com

"Muy Bueno" Tortilla Soup

2 tablespoons olive oil
1 cup chopped yellow or white onion
2 teaspoons chopped garlic
1½ teaspoons salt
1½ teaspoons cumin
1 tablespoon tomato paste
6 cups low-sodium chicken broth
1 pound shredded chicken
Black pepper
Vegetable oil
6 corn tortillas
1 to 2 cups 4-cheese or Mexican shredded cheese
2 Hass avocados, diced
½ cup sour cream
½ to 1 cup cilantro leaves, to taste
2 limes

In a large heavy pot, heat olive oil at medium high heat. Add onions, garlic, salt and cumin. Add tomato paste and cook 1 to 2 minutes stirring continuously. Add broth and bring to a simmer. Simmer 20 to 25 minutes. Season shredded chicken with salt and pepper to taste. Add chicken to broth and continue to simmer 5 to 10 minutes. While the chicken and broth are simmering, pour some vegetable oil into a shallow pan for frying tortilla strips. Pour enough oil to reach ½ inch. Heat at medium heat until very hot but not smoking. Slice corn tortillas into thin strips. Fry strips in batches until crisp. Drain on a paper towel. Set aside. To Serve: Assemble 4 to 6 serving bowls in a row. Pour soup into each bowl leaving 1 to 2 inches on top for garnishes. Take a handful of shredded cheese and place it in the center of each bowl. Then pile crispy tortilla strips, diced avocado, a dollop of sour cream and whole cilantro leaves on top of the cheese. Add a splash of lime juice all over the soup and garnishes right before serving. Delicioso!!

The Village/El Pueblo Staff, Biloxi

Homemade Chicken Soup

1 whole chicken, cut-up
2 cans tomato soup
½ cup milk
½ stick butter
4 tablespoons sugar
1 onion, diced
1 can whole-kernel corn
1 can creamed corn
1 can Rotel (mild)
Salt and pepper
1 (16-ounce) package spaghetti

Boil chicken, saving broth. In large saucepan or medium stockpot, put equal parts broth and tomato soup. Add milk, butter, sugar and onion. Bring to a boil while de-boning chicken. Once broth is at a full rolling boil, add corn, Rotel and chicken. Season to taste. Bring to rolling boil again and add spaghetti. Once noodles are done, it is ready.

D. J., Lena

Smack Ya! White Chili

2 pounds lean ground turkey or chicken
1 onion, chopped
2 (4-ounce) cans green chilies, drained
1 cup chicken broth
3 teaspoons chili powder
1 teaspoon garlic powder
3 cans great Northern beans, undrained
1 can whole-kernel corn, divided
Salt and pepper to taste
1½ cups water
Flour or Cornmeal to thicken, if needed

Brown meat with onions and chilies. Move to a covered pan and add remaining ingredients. Simmer on low at least 1 hour. Stir carefully and no more often than necessary to keep beans whole. Serve over crushed white tortilla chips and splash with hot sauce, if desired.

The Marcus Lee Family, USM

Crossroads Chili Cook-Off
First Saturday in April • Corinth

An International Chili Society sanctioned event, the Crossroads Chili Festival hosts chili cookers from all over the nation who are vying for red chili, green chili and salsa championships. There is free entertainment all day and local vendors are on hand selling items that are handmade or homegrown within a 100 mile radius. A Peoples Choice tasting contest is featured from 11 a.m. until 1 p.m. and the hot pepper eating contest is not to be missed.

800.748.9048 • crossroadsfestival.corinth.net

Broccoli-Cheese Soup

1 (10-ounce) package frozen broccoli, chopped
1 (15-ounce) can chicken broth
2 teaspoons (or 2 cubes) chicken bouillon
½ cup chopped onion
½ cup chopped celery
Pepper to taste
½ cup milk
2 tablespoons butter or margarine
3 tablespoons cornstarch (with enough milk to dissolve)
2½ to 3 cups shredded Cheddar cheese (or Velveeta)

Boil first 5 ingredients until barely tender. Purée in blender about 3 seconds. Add pepper. Return to heat. Add milk, butter and cornstarch mixture. Blend and stir until hot. Add cheese. Cook until thickened, stirring constantly. Do not boil.

Turnip Green Soup

2 tablespoons oil
1 large onion, finely chopped
3 cans chicken broth
3 large potatoes, peeled and cubed
3 cans great Northern beans
1 (8-ounce) package chopped ham
1 (16-ounce) package frozen turnip greens

Sauté onions in oil. Add broth and potatoes and bring to boil. Add remaining ingredients; bring back to boil. Cover and simmer 3 hours. Serve with sweet potatoes and cornbread.

Anita Musgrove, Brandon

Creamy Potato Cheese Soup

1 medium onion, chopped
2 medium carrots, coarsely grated
¾ teaspoon salt
½ teaspoon black pepper
½ teaspoon paprika
½ teaspoon dry mustard
1 pound potatoes, peeled and cut in ½-inch cubes
29 ounces vegetable broth
½ cup fat-free half and half
8 ounces Cheddar or colby cheese

Coat a nonstick medium pot with cooking spray and set over medium heat. Cook onions until they just begin to color. Add carrots, salt, pepper, paprika and mustard. Mix well and continue to cook until carrots begin to soften. Add potatoes, broth and half-and-half. Increase heat and bring to a boil, then reduce heat to simmer. Cook until potatoes are tender, about 20 minutes. Add cheese and stir to melt; purée in batches in a blender. Serve with toasted bread, croutons or crackers.

Stephanie Jackson, Faulkner

© Alessio Cola • image from istockphoto.com

Anita's Crockpot Potato Soup

2 (8-ounce) packages cream cheese
3 cans cream of chicken soup
3 cans chicken broth
1 bag cubed hash brown potatoes
1 package bacon, fried crispy and crumbled

Place cream cheese in crockpot on low; stir frequently until melted. Increase heat to medium. Add soup, broth and potatoes; stir well. Cook 1 hour or longer. About 30 minutes before serving, add bacon and set crockpot to low.

Samantha Williamson, Golden

Red Skin Potato Salad

2 pounds red skin potatoes
¾ to 1 cup mayonnaise
½ cup finely chopped green onions
1 envelope dry ranch dressing mix
1½ cups bacon pieces
1 (8-ounce) package shredded sharp Cheddar cheese

Wash and cube potatoes (with skin on). Boil in water to cover until done; drain. Combine ¾ cup mayonnaise, onions and ranch. Stir into potatoes. Mix well using additional mayonnaise if desired or needed. Top with bacon pieces and cheese. Best served chilled.

Mary Beemon, Good Hope

Biloxi Bay Potato Salad

1 pound boiled Mississippi Gulf Shrimp,
   cleaned and peeled (small to medium)
6 to 8 medium potatoes, boiled whole just until done (don't over-cook)
5 to 6 green onions, chopped
2 stalks celery, finely chopped
4 to 5 eggs, boiled and chopped
1 cup sweet relish
1 tablespoon prepared mustard
1 cup salad dressing (mayonnaise based)
Cajun seasoning, to taste
Salt and pepper, to taste

Cut boiled potatoes in pieces (about 1-inch; not too small). Combine all ingredients and serve.
Great served with gumbo.

Irvin Jackson,
Mississippi Department of Marine Resources

© Ruslan Olinchuk • Image from bigstockphoto.com

Honey Dijon Bacon Potato Salad

5 cups cooked and quartered baby Yukon gold potatoes
1 medium red onion, diced
1½ cups diced celery
1 cup cooked drained and chopped bacon
2 tablespoons honey
2 tablespoons mayonnaise
1 tablespoon Dijon mustard
1 tablespoon Creole mustard
1 tablespoon chopped fresh parsley
Salt and pepper to taste
Hot sauce to taste

Combine all ingredients; mix well. Adjust seasoning with salt, pepper and hot sauce. Cover and refrigerate. Serve with Catfish Institute Mississippi Cajun Catfish (page 156).

The Catfish Institute, Jackson

Macaroni Salad

4 cups elbow pasta,
  cooked and drained
1 cucumber, chopped
1/3 cup bacon bits
2/3 cup mayonnaise
2 tablespoons milk
1 tablespoon parsley
1 teaspoon onion powder
1 teaspoon celery seed
Salt and pepper to taste

Mix all of the ingredients together in a big bowl. Refrigerate until ready to serve.

Lebanese Salad

1 pound red potatoes,
   about 4
½ cup chopped fresh parsley, washed
2 tablespoons chopped fresh mint leaves
Lettuce
1 tomato, cut in wedges

Dressing:

2 cloves garlic, crushed
3 tablespoons olive oil
3 large lemons, juiced
Salt to taste

Rinse potatoes, scrubbing off any spots with a potato brush. Place potatoes in a large pot covered with cold water to about 1 inch above potatoes and bring to a boil, uncovered, over high heat. Reduce heat to medium-low and simmer potatoes until just tender, about 15 minutes. Drain and cool. While potatoes are cooling, combine all dressing ingredients; chill until ready to serve. Peel and dice potatoes into serving bowl. Add parsley and mint; toss with dressing. Chill until ready to serve. Before serving, toss again. Spoon onto lettuce leaves and garnish with tomato wedges. Yield: 4 servings

Shirley A. Glaab, Hattiesburg

Healthy Mardis Gras Pasta Salad

1 package Splenda
¼ cup fresh raspberries
½ pound whole wheat fusilli or rotini pasta
½ pound tri-colored fusilli or rotini pasta
½ small onion, chopped
1 tablespoon minced garlic
1 tablespoon extra virgin olive oil
1½ pounds skinless, boneless chicken breast, chopped
1 (8-ounce) bag frozen sweet peas
3 carrots, shredded
½ red bell pepper, diced
⅓ yellow bell pepper, diced
⅓ green bell pepper, diced
1½ cups halved fresh grape tomatoes
½ cup green pitted olives
3 tablespoons cilantro
½ cup mandarin oranges
⅓ cup dried cranberries
⅓ cup halved unsalted cashews
5 to 6 tablespoons Wishbone olive oil vinaigrette dressing
¼ teaspoon McCormick 1 Step Garlic Herb Chicken Seasoning
¼ cup chopped radicchio

Ever since we moved to Biloxi, Mardis Gras has been a special time of year. It is fun to make dishes that remind us of Mardis Gras, and this pasta salad never fails to transport us to a Biloxi Mardis Gras parade on the square. The fabulous colors of purple, gold and green make this meal as pretty as it is tasty. It's a spectacular salad which is great year around, but best served at Mardis Gras. In our house, it is a summer staple!

Sprinkle Splenda over raspberries and set aside. Cook both pastas according to package directions; combine and set aside. Add onion and garlic to a pan with olive oil. Add chicken and sauté until no longer pink. Cook peas until warm and set aside. Combine remaining ingredients in large bowl. Add chicken, raspberries, pasta and peas; toss gently. Enjoy!

Maureen Wagner, Biloxi

Marinated Rice Salad

2 packages chicken-flavored rice
2 (6-ounce) jars marinated artichoke hearts
½ cup mayonnaise
½ green bell pepper, chopped
8 green onions, chopped (with tops if not too strong)
16 pimento-stuffed olives, sliced
1 teaspoon curry powder
Salt and pepper

Cook rice as directed, omitting butter; set aside to cool. Drain artichokes, reserving marinade, and slice. Combine marinade and mayonnaise. Add artichokes, peppers, onions, olives and curry powder. Salt and pepper to taste; mix well. Stir in rice and chill until ready to serve. Serves 12. (This recipe can easily be halved to serve 4 to 6 people.)

Donna Monroe, Greenville

Granny's Chicken Salad

2 cups cubed cooked chicken
1 cup chopped celery
½ cup crushed pecans
½ cup sliced olives
2 hard-boiled eggs
½ cup mayonnaise
Juice of half lemon

Combine all ingredients and mix well. Add or reduce mayonnaise, as desired. Serve chilled.

Harriett Whitaker, Grenada

Chicken Salad

1 whole chicken, boiled,
   de-boned and shredded
1 small bunch purple grapes,
   finely chopped
2 large red apples, finely chopped
1 medium yellow onion, finely chopped
2 celery stalks, finely chopped
1 cup mayo
   (more if you like it creamier)
Salt and pepper to taste

Combine all ingredients and refrigerate 1 hour or until ready to serve. Excellent on a bed of lettuce, in a sandwich, or with crackers as an hors d'oeuvres.

Melissa Webb, Ludlow

Hometown Chicken Salad

2 large cans chicken, drained
1 (8-ounce) jar dill pickle relish
8 eggs, boiled and chopped
1 bunch green onions, chopped
Blue Plate mayonnaise, to taste
Salt and Pepper, to taste

This is really better if you let it set overnight and is always a hit with everyone.

Mash chicken with a fork until completely separated. Stir in remaining ingredients. Chill 2 hours or longer before serving. Serve with crackers as an appetizer, as a sandwich or on a bed of shredded lettuce.

Rose Compere, Mendenhall

Watergate Salad

1 box pistachio pudding mix
1 can crushed pineapple
1 (8-ounce) tub Cool Whip
½ bag miniature marshmallows
1 cup chopped pecans

Mix together; chill before serving.

Joy Sumerall, Raymond

Blueberry Chutney Salad

1 tablespoon olive oil
1 small onion, finally chopped (about ¼ cup)
2 pints blueberries, washed
1 tablespoon sugar
Pinch each ground cinnamon, cloves, allspice,
   fresh ground black pepper
2 tablespoons red wine or balsamic vinegar
1 bag spinach, rinsed and dried
   (or other preferred salad greens)
3 strips bacon, fried and crumbled
6 to 8 ounces feta or goat cheese, cut into small chunks

Sauté onion in pan with oil. Add blueberries, sugar and spices; shake the pan while cooking. Add vinegar and cook a few minutes until juice thickens to a nice sauce. Prepare salad greens in a bowl, arranging bacon and cheese on top. Serve immediately while chutney is still warm; pour over top of lettuce.

Gulf South Blueberry Growers,
Pearl River Blues Organic Farm, Lumberton

Baked Fruit Salad

1 can peaches
1 can pineapple chunks
1 can pears
1 cup berries (blueberries, blackberries, raspberries,
    whatever you have handy)
1 cup brown sugar
½ teaspoon allspice
½ teaspoon cinnamon
Dash cloves
1 tablespoon flour

Drain all fruit. Combine in a baking dish; stir in brown sugar. Combine spices and flour and sprinkle over top. Bake at 300° for 30 to 45 minutes. For a side dish, serve warm or chilled. For a dessert, serve in a bowl topped with whipped cream or along with ice cream.

Harriett Whitaker, Grenada

MawMaw's Easy Peach Salad

1 can peach pie filling
1 can crushed pineapple, drained
1 box frozen strawberries
3 bananas, sliced

Mix all together and serve immediately.

Anita Williamson, Golden

Birthday Surprise

2 tomatoes, chopped
1 small can pineapple tidbits
2 banana peppers, chopped
¼ cup Italian dressing
1 carrot, chopped
3 tablespoons Cool Whip

My son Nicholas surprised me with this recipe one night on my birthday. Like a good Momma, I ate every bite. Nicholas requested that his recipe be included in this cookbook. Be sure to make it if you want to really surprise someone you love. – Sheila

Combine tomatoes, pineapple and banana peppers in a bowl; mix well. Top with Italian dressing. Serve with carrots and Cool Whip on the side.

Petrified Forest
Flora

© Nic Williams

Grape Salad

2 pounds seedless grapes
1 (8-ounce) package cream cheese, softened
1 (8-ounce) carton sour cream
1 teaspoon vanilla extract
1 cup chopped pecans
1 cup brown sugar

Great for a salad or a dessert.

Wash grapes and set aside to dry. Combine cream cheese, sour cream and vanilla; add grapes. Top with brown sugar and pecans.

Delores McMillian, Clinton

Creamy Grape Salad

4 pounds seedless grapes,
**   green or red**
2 packages cream cheese, softened
1 (16-ounce) carton sour cream
¼ cup sugar
1½ cups chopped pecans or walnuts

Rinse grapes; drain. Combine cream cheese, sour cream and sugar. Stir in grapes and nuts. Chill before serving.

Harriett Whitaker, Grenada

Crunchy Romaine Toss

Sweet and Sour Dressing:

1 cup vegetable oil
1 cup sugar
½ cup red wine vinegar (or balsamic vinegar)
3 teaspoons soy sauce
Salt and pepper to taste

A tangy, crunchy salad that beats a generic tossed salad any day. We serve this at all holiday gatherings. It's a winner!

Salad:

1 cup pecans
1 package Ramen noodles,
   uncooked, and broken up (discard flavor packet)
½ stick butter
1 bunch broccoli, coarsely chopped
1 head romaine lettuce, washed and broken into pieces
4 green onions, chopped

Blend all dressing ingredients and shake well; set aside. Brown pecans and noodles in butter. Drain and cool on paper towels. Combine with broccoli, romaine and onions. Just before serving, shake Sweet and Sour Dressing again to mix well; pour over salad. Toss to coat well. Leftover dressing will keep several weeks in the refrigerator.

Pam Simpson, Vancleave

Country Boy Steak Salad

Steak:

½ teaspoon garlic powder
½ teaspoon brown sugar
½ teaspoon ground red pepper
¼ teaspoon salt
¼ teaspoon black pepper
1 (1-pound) boneless sirloin steak, trimmed

Heat a nonstick grill pan over medium-high heat. Combine all ingredients, except steak. Rub into both sides of steak. Coat grill pan with nonstick cooking spray. Cook steak to desired heat, about 4 minutes for medium. Remove from pan; allow to rest 5 minutes before slicing (very important). Cut steak diagonally across grain into thin slices. Allow to rest again while preparing salad.

Salad:

4 slices sourdough bread, ½-inch thick
2 tablespoons butter, softened
Garlic powder to taste
1½ cups chopped tomatoes
1 cucumber, thinly sliced
½ red onion, thinly sliced
1 (16-ounce) bag classic iceberg salad mix
**   (or 1 head iceberg lettuce chopped and rinsed well)**
½ to 1 cup ranch dressing

Place bread slices on a baking sheet. Spread butter over one side and sprinkle with garlic powder. Broil 2 minutes on each side or until lightly browned; but into cubes. Combine bread cubes, tomatoes, cucumber, onions and lettuce in a large bowl. Add dressing and toss well. Divide salad evenly among 4 plates; top with steak. Serves 4.

Spinach and Strawberry Poppy Seed Salad

Sesame-Poppy Seed Dressing:

1 cup sugar
½ cup cider vinegar
1 tablespoon minced onion
½ teaspoon Worcestershire sauce
¼ teaspoon salt
1 cup vegetable oil
¼ cup sesame seeds, toasted
2 tablespoons poppy seeds

I make this salad all the time and people rave over it.

Pulse first 5 ingredients in a blender 2 or 3 times or until smooth. With blender running, add oil in a slow, steady stream; process until smooth. Stir in season and poppy seeds; chill 24 hours.

Salad:

2 (6-ounce) packages fresh baby spinach
2 pints fresh strawberries, sliced

Topping options:

Chopped cooked bacon
Chopped fresh broccoli
Blanched sugar snap peas
Sliced red onion

Combine baby spinach and strawberries in a large bowl; toss with ½ cup Sesame-Poppy Seed Dressing just before serving. Serve remaining dressing and desired toppings on the side.

Demaris Lee, Petal

Mom's Mississippi Cornbread Salad

1 (8½-ounce) box cornbread mix,
   plus ingredients to prepare per package directions
1 (1-ounce) ranch-style salad dressing mix
1 (8-ounce) carton sour cream
1 cup mayonnaise
2 cans pinto beans, drained
½ cup chopped red bell pepper
½ cup chopped green bell pepper
½ cup chopped onion
2 cans whole-kernel corn
3 large tomatoes, chopped
1 (16-ounce) package bacon, cooked and crumbled
2 cups shredded cheese

This recipe is submitted in honor of my mother, Imogene Furlong. It's easy to prepare and is great for parties and potluck dinners.

Prepare cornbread per package directions; cool. Mix dressing mix, sour cream and mayonnaise; set aside. Crumble ½ of the cornbread in dish. Layer with 1 can pinto beans, ½ of the chopped pepper, ½ of the chopped onion and 1 can corn. Continue layers with ½ of the tomatoes, ½ dressing mix, ½ bacon and ½ cheese. Repeat layers. Cover and chill 3 hours.

Stephanie Jackson, Faulkner

Broccoli Salad

1 cup mayonnaise
4 tablespoons sugar
   (sugar substitute can be used)
1 tablespoon apple cider vinegar
4 cups chopped fresh broccoli
1 small onion, chopped
½ cup raisins
5 slices bacon, cooked and crumbled

Mix mayonnaise, sugar and vinegar together. Toss in remaining ingredients; chill and serve.

Teresa Vanlandingham, Brandon

Broccoli Salad Mold

2 packages frozen broccoli
1 can beef consommé
2 envelopes unflavored gelatin
1 (8-ounce) package cream cheese, softened
1 cup mayonnaise
4 eggs, boiled and chopped
2 tablespoons Real Lemon brand lemon juice
1½ teaspoons salt
1 small jar pimento, drained
1 teaspoon chopped bell pepper
3 tablespoons Worcestershire sauce
1 tablespoon Tabasco sauce

Cook broccoli; drain well. Heat beef consommé; add gelatin and stir until fully dissolved. Combine cream cheese and mayonnaise. Add broccoli, beef gelatin and remaining ingredients. Pour into greased mold. Refrigerate. Makes approximately 6 cups. This may be frozen. I always double this recipe.

Rita S. Franklin, Hattiesburg

Corn Salad

2 cans shoe peg corn
1 small onion, chopped
1 bell pepper, chopped
1 tomato, chopped
2½ tablespoons mayo
Salt and pepper to taste

This is a favorite of my daughter, not because of how it tastes, but because she says it looks pretty in the bowl.

Mix all ingredients in a pretty serving bowl; stir well. Chill before serving.

Joy Sumerall, Raymond

Southern Soul Bean Salad

2 cups cooked or canned navy,
    great northern, or small white beans
2 cups cooked or canned dark or light kidney beans
2 cups cooked or canned garbanzo beans
1½ cups vinaigrette dressing
1 tablespoon hot sauce
½ tablespoon vinegar
Salt and pepper to taste
1 cup crispy onion rings
Tomato wedges

A delicious Soul Food side dish that goes great with pork, chicken and, of course, greens.

Drain beans and mix together. Add dressing, hot sauce, vinegar, salt and pepper. Stir to mix. Refrigerate at least 1 hour (or more). When ready to serve, mix again. Taste and add more seasoning and vinegar, if necessary. Toss with onion rings just before serving. Garnish with tomato wedges.

The Marcus Lee Family, USM

Vegetables &
Other Side Dishes

Glazed Carrots page 98

Cathy's Bread & Butter Pickles

6 pounds pickling cucumbers (4 to 5 inches long)
2 pounds small onions, sliced thin
½ cup pickling salt
4½ cups apple cider vinegar
3 cups sugar
1½ teaspoons ground turmeric
1 teaspoon celery seeds
2 teaspoons yellow mustard seeds

Gently wash cucumbers and remove blossom ends. Slice cucumbers crosswise ¼ inches thick. In a large bowl, toss cucumbers and onions with salt. Cover vegetables with ice cubes from 2 to 3 ice trays. Let vegetables stand 3 to 4 hours. Drain vegetables. In a large non-reactive pot, bring remaining ingredients to a boil. Add vegetables, and slowly bring contents to a boil. Using a slotted spoon, pack vegetables loosely in 8 pint-sized jars or 4 quart-sized mason jars, leaving ½ inch headspace. Divide liquid evenly among jars. Close jars with hot two-piece caps. To ensure a good seal, process jars 10 minutes in a boiling-water bath. Store cooled jars in a cool, dry, dark place at least 3 weeks before eating pickles. Makes about 4 quarts.

Cathy Updegraff, Tupelo

© Kent Whitaker

Marinated Cucumbers

8 cups sliced cucumbers
1 cup chopped onion
1 cup vinegar
2 cups sugar
1 tablespoon salt (less if desired)
1 teaspoon celery seed

Layer cucumbers and onion in wide-mouthed jar with lid. Combine vinegar, sugar, salt and celery seed; mix well. Pour over cucumbers and onions. Place in refrigerator. Will keep indefinitely.

Dean Linville

Grandma Glover's Chili Sauce

12 tomatoes, chopped
4 onions, chopped
3 pods peppers
   (hot, sweet and/or banana peppers)
1 cup sugar
2 cups vinegar
1 tablespoon black pepper
1 tablespoon salt

Heat in a large stockpot. Cook over medium-low heat, stirring frequently, until sauce gets thick as you want. Pour in hot jars and seal.

Betty Davis, Fulton

Fried Green Tomatoes

1 large egg, lightly beaten
½ cup buttermilk
½ cup all-purpose flour
1 teaspoon salt
1 teaspoon pepper
1 cup seasoned stuffing crumbs
3 medium green tomatoes, cut into ⅓-inch thick slices
Vegetable oil
Salt and pepper to taste

Combine eggs and buttermilk; set aside. Combine flour, salt and pepper in a shallow pan and set aside. Put stuffing in another shallow pan. Dredge sliced tomatoes in flour, then egg and buttermilk, then stuffing to coat both sides. Pour oil in large cast-iron skillet. Heat to 375°. Drop breaded tomatoes in oil and cook until golden, about 2 minutes per side. Drain on paper towels and season with salt and pepper while hot. Serves 4 to 6.

Mrs. Holcombe's Hot Green Tomatoes

White vinegar, enough to fill jars
2 pounds green tomatoes
10 to 12 jalapeño peppers, chopped with ½ seeds
5 to 6 teaspoons coarse salt
5 to 6 pint-size jars

Choose firm, small to medium green tomatoes (entirely green, not partially ripe). Bring vinegar to boil. While waiting for vinegar to boil, wash tomatoes well; remove stem ends. Slice tomatoes and place into pint-size jars. Into each jar add 2 chopped jalapeño peppers with ½ seeds and 1 teaspoon coarse salt. Ladle hot boiling vinegar into jars and seal. Leave sealed about 2 to 3 weeks, then ENJOY! Makes 5 to 6 pints.

Mrs. Holcombe

Mississippi Blues Fried Okra

1 pound okra
Milk for dredging
Hot sauce to taste
½ cup all purpose flour
½ cup cornmeal
Black pepper to taste
Creole seasoning to taste

This recipe is about the only way I cook okra. The trick is to use just a bit of hot sauce and Creole seasoning for a smooth mellow flavor with a touch of heat. Like a smooth blues song!

Rinse okra and cut in bite-size pieces. Place in a bowl with milk and a few dashes of hot sauce. In another bowl, combine flour, cornmeal, black pepper and seasoning. Dredge okra in dry mixture and fry in hot oil until browned. Drain on paper towels. You can sprinkle with a bit more Creole seasoning just as they are placed on the paper towel, if desired. (Some people add onion to the oil for flavor. If I do, I add 1 good-size slice at a time of sweet onion. When it starts to burn, I replace that slice with a new one. That way tiny pieces of burnt onion are not stuck to your okra.)

Belinda Johnston, Mississippi State

© David Gilder • image from bigstockphoto.com

Squash Casserole

1½ pounds squash
1 stick butter
1 box cornbread stuffing mix
½ cup chopped onion
½ pint sour cream
1 can cream of chicken soup

This casserole is a great dish to serve at Thanksgiving.

Cook squash in small amount of salted water until tender; drain. Melt butter in a 2-quart casserole dish. Reserve ½ dry stuffing mix for topping; stir the remaining stuffing mix into butter. Pour squash over breadcrumbs. Sprinkle chopped onion over the squash mixture. Combine sour cream and soup; spread over squash and onion. Sprinkle remaining crumbs on top. Bake at 350° for about 30 minutes or until bubbly.

Rose Compere, Mendenhall

Roast N Boast
Last Weekend of August • Columbus

Our contest is a Memphis Bar-B-Q Network sanctioned contest. Teams from across the Southeast come that weekend to compete for prize money and points. We also have a local or "backyard" competition. We have live entertainment at night and many vendors throughout the weekend.

662.549.5054 • roastnboast.com

© David Smith • image from bigstockphoto.com

Squash Delight

2 cups cubed yellow squash
1 onion, finely chopped
1 bell pepper, chopped
½ cup mayonnaise
½ stick margarine, softened
1 egg, beaten
4 ounces cheese
   (shredded Cheddar or Velveeta)
1½ teaspoons sugar
¼ teaspoon garlic salt
Salt and pepper to taste
2 to 3 cups crushed crackers

This recipe will cause confirmed squash-haters to discover a new-found love for it.

Cook squash, onion and bell pepper in water to cover until tender. Drain and mash. Stir in mayonnaise, margarine, egg, cheese, sugar and garlic salt. Season to taste and mix well. Pour into treated casserole dish. Top with crushed crackers. Bake at 350° about 35 to 45 minutes or until set.

Tory Hackett, Morton

Asparagus Casserole

1 sleeve saltine crackers, crushed
1 can cream of mushroom soup
½ pound sharp Cheddar cheese, grated
1 can asparagus spears, drained
¼ cup milk
2 tablespoons butter
Paprika, optional

My niece Pam loves this dish. I fix it for lunches at the office, too.

Grease 1-quart casserole dish. Cover bottom with a layer of cracker crumbs. Layer ½ can mushroom soup, then layer grated cheese (use about ½). Layer asparagus then another cheese layer. Finish with a layer of remaining soup and the remaining cracker crumbs. Pour ¼ cup milk over top and 3 or 4 dabs butter. Before baking, sprinkle with paprika if desired. (This can be left in refrigerator for a day in advance before cooking; add 15 minutes to baking time.) Bake uncovered 30 to 40 minutes at 350º or microwave uncovered on high until bubbly, 5 to 10 minutes.

Alice M. Henderson, Florence

Eggplant Supreme

1 pound ground beef
1 small onion, chopped
1 medium eggplant
1 (16-ounce) box Spanish rice
1 pound tomatoes
1 (2-ounce) can mushrooms, drained
1 cup grated cheese

Brown beef and onion over medium heat; drain. Peel and dice eggplant. Cook in boiling salted water until tender; drain. Combine ground beef, eggplant, Spanish rice, tomatoes and drained mushrooms. Pour into greased 1½ quart casserole. Spread with cheese. Bake at 350º for about 1 hour until golden brown. Makes 6 to 8 servings.

Annie Lou Shaw

Lisa's Cabbage Casserole

1 head cabbage, washed and chopped fine
1 onion, thinly sliced
Salt and pepper
2 to 3 potatoes,
    washed, peeled and sliced in circles
2 pounds hamburger meat
Tony Chachere's Creole seasoning
1 can Rotel tomatoes
1 can cream of chicken soup
1 can cream of mushroom soup
1 pound smoked sausage, sliced in rounds

This is a great family meal served with a pan of cornbread. I usually make it for large crowds - deer camp suppers or when friends and family are coming for supper.

Preheat oven to 450°. This makes a LARGE pan; I use a disposable aluminum baking pan. Spread cabbage in bottom of pan. Layer on onions. Salt and pepper to taste. Layer potatoes over onions and sprinkle with Creole seasoning. Brown ground beef; drain. Spread over potatoes. Combine Rotel tomatoes and both soups; pour over ground beef. Spread smoked sausage rounds over top. Cover dish with tinfoil and cook in oven about 1 hour. When potatoes are tender, it is done.

Southern Soul Mustard Greens

4 bunches leaf mustard greens
Water for boiling
1 ham bone
Meat from 1 smoked turkey leg
1 tablespoon salt
1 tablespoon black pepper
1 onion, cut in half
Dash hot sauce

Remove stems from greens; rinse, drain, rinse again and drain well. Cut into smaller pieces as desired. In a big pot, boil meat about 45 minutes with salt and pepper. Add greens and simmer 1 hour. Add onion and hot sauce about 30 minutes before serving.

The Marcus Lee Family. Southern Miss Golden Eagles

Glazed Carrots

1 pound (about 7 medium) carrots,
    peeled and cut ¼-inch thick at an angle
2 tablespoons butter
½ teaspoon salt
1 cup ginger ale
½ teaspoon chili powder
1 tablespoon parsley, optional

In a sauté pan over medium heat, combine carrots, butter, salt and ginger ale. Cover and bring to a good simmer. Stir, reduce heat to low and cook 5 minutes still covered. Remove lid and add chili powder. Increase heat to high. Cook, stirring frequently, until ginger ale is reduced to a glaze, approximately 4 to 5 minutes. Sprinkle with parsley before serving. Serve immediately. Serves 4 to 6.

Southern Style Greens

**3½ to 4 pounds collard, turnip or
    mustard greens (or a mixture)**
½ pound lean salt pork or smoked ham hock
1 tablespoon sugar
3 beef boullion cubes
8 cups water
1 tablespoon margarine
Salt and pepper

Wash greens repeatedly until all grit is removed–it will take a lot of washing.
Drain. Remove and discard large stems. Combine pork, sugar, bouillon
cubes, water and margarine in a large soup pot. Bring to a boil over medium-
high heat. Boil 5 to 10 minutes. Add greens. Reduce heat and simmer,
covered, for 1½ hours or until greens are tender. Add salt and pepper to
taste. Makes 8 to 10 servings.

© Mi.Ti. • image from bigstockphoto.com

Candied Sweet Potatoes

2 large sweet potatoes
1 tablespoon baking soda
¾ cup sugar
¼ teaspoon salt
3 tablespoons butter

Peel sweet potatoes and cut in circles about ½-inch thick. Cover with warm water; stir in baking soda. Soak 10 minutes; drain in colander and rinse. Combine sugar, salt and ½ cup water in a saucepan; bring to a low boil. Add potatoes and continue to cook, stirring syrup over potatoes, until syrup is thick and potatoes are done. Melt butter over potatoes, stir, and serve. Serves 3 to 4.

Vardaman Sweet Potato Festival
First Saturday in November • Vardaman

This annual event kicks off with Arts and Crafts Day which generates lots of excitement with crowds of 10,000 to 20,000 people. Opening day also includes a 5K run/walk, political speakers, sweet potato critter contest, a pie eating contest, live entertainment and much more. The week-long celebration continues with the Sweet Potato King & Queen Beauty Pageants and more during the week. The second Saturday closes the harvest celebration with an original sweet potato recipe contest and the Sweet Potato Banquet. Join us in the "Sweet Potato Capital of the World" for old-fashioned family fun.

662.682.7559 • vardamansweetpotatofestival.org

Sweet Potato Casserole

1 cup packed brown sugar
1 cup chopped pecans
½ cup self-rising flour
½ cup (1 stick) butter, melted (divided)
3 cups mashed cooked sweet potatoes
1 cup sugar
2 eggs, lightly beaten
1 teaspoon vanilla
¼ cup heavy whipping cream

Combine brown sugar, pecans, flour and ¼ cup melted butter; stir together with fork and set aside for topping. Combine sweet potatoes, sugar, eggs and vanilla with a fork; add heavy cream. Spoon into a large casserole dish. Cover with reserved topping and bake at 350° for 20 to 30 minutes or until topping is golden brown. Serves 6 to 8.

Alexis Rather, Oxford

Roasted Parmesan Potatoes

10 red potatoes, washed
Olive oil
2 tablespoon chives
1 package dry ranch dressing mix
½ cup Parmesan cheese
   plus more for topping
Salt and pepper

Cut potatoes in thin circles. Drizzle with olive oil; stir. Add chives, dry ranch mix and cheese; stir. Cover bottom of a large roasting pan with olive oil. Spread potatoes in pan. Salt and pepper to taste. Sprinkle with additional Parmesan cheese, if desired. Bake at 350° for 1 hour or until potatoes are tender.

Melissa Webb, Ludlow

Crab Stuffed Potatoes

6 baking potatoes
¼ pound (1 stick) butter
1 teaspoon salt
½ teaspoon black pepper
½ teaspoon Zatarain's seasoning
4 teaspoons grated onion
8 ounces (1 cup) sour cream
1 cup shredded Cheddar cheese
1 cup fresh crabmeat
    or ½ pound frozen crabmeat

Bake potatoes in 350° oven until done. Cut potatoes in half length-wise and carefully scoop out potato to save shells. Add butter, salt, pepper, Zatarain's® and onion to potato pulp and coarsely mix. Add sour cream and blend. Fold in cheese and crab. Spoon into potato shells. Bake 350° for 15 minutes. Can freeze separately in freezer bags. Bake at 350° for 30 to 40 minutes or microwave 4 to 6 minutes. Fluff potatoes with fork mid-way while cooking to keep center of potato from erupting.

Valerie Mabry, Biloxi

Cheesy Ranch Mashed Potatoes

5 pounds potatoes, peeled and cubed
1 tablespoon butter
¼ cup sour cream
¼ cup imitation or Real bacon bits
1 envelope ranch dressing mix
Salt and pepper to taste
2 cups shredded Cheddar cheese

This recipe came to me from one of my husband's friends. I make this for barbecue parties with friends and family.

Boil potatoes until very soft; drain. Preheat oven to 300°. Mash potatoes with an electric mixer. Add butter and sour cream and continue to beat until creamy. Stir in bacon and ranch dressing mix. Season to taste with salt and pepper; mix well. Spread in a glass baking dish treated with nonstick spray. Sprinkle cheese on top. Bake about 15 minutes or until cheese is melted.

Krista Griffin, Carthage

Skillet Potato Pie

1 pound potatoes
3 tablespoons chopped chives
1 teaspoon salt, divided
3 eggs, beaten
¼ cup light cream
¼ cup grated Parmesan cheese
Dash pepper
4 tablespoons butter or margarine

Peel and shred potatoes. Add chives and ½ teaspoon salt; mix eggs, cream, cheese, ½ teaspoon salt and pepper. Reserve. Heat 2 tablespoons butter in a 10-inch non-stick skillet over medium heat. Add potatoes, shaping into a patty. Reduce heat to low. Cook about 10 minutes, or until potatoes are brown. Invert potato patty onto a platter. Heat remaining butter in skillet until hot. Slide potato patty back into skillet, and cook 8 more minutes, or until brown. Cut into wedges and garnish.

Magnolia Hominy Bake

2 (1-pound 13-ounce) cans white hominy
2 (4-ounce) cans green chilies, minced
Salt to taste
⅛ teaspoon white pepper
Sour cream
Butter
½ cup whipping cream
1 cup grated Monterey jack cheese

Drain and rinse hominy. Butter a 2½-3 quart casserole. Layer ingredients in following order: hominy, green chilies, season with salt and pepper, dot with sour cream and butter, repeat layers, ending with hominy. Pour whipping cream on top. Dot the top with butter and sour cream all over. Sprinkle with cheese. Bake at 350° for 25 to 30 minutes.

Donna Monroe, Greenville

Succotash with a Twist

5 to 6 slices bacon
1 medium onion, diced
1 cup red bell pepper, diced
1 cup soy beans
1½ cups corn
½ cup butter
½ cup heavy cream
¾ cup Parmesan cheese
1 tablespoon parsley

Cook bacon in pan and remove before it is cooked crispy. Add onion and pepper to drippings and cook until tender. Add soy beans and corn. Cut or chop bacon in small pieces and return to pan with vegetables. Cover and allow to simmer while you prepare your sauce. In a saucepan, melt butter. Add cream and cook until hot but not boiling. Add cheese and parsley; stir until mixture is smooth. Pour sauce over vegetable mix and bring up heat until heated through.

Stephen Stolk, Brandon

Aunt Ceil's Mississippi-Must Fried Corn

4 ears field corn (not sweet),
   shucked and silked
2 tablespoons bacon drippings
2 tablespoons butter
Salt and pepper

Cut corn with big side of a 4-sided grater (or carefully with a sharp knife). Do this over a large bowl. Scrape ear with butter knife to get more goodie out. Heat bacon drippings and butter in large skillet until butter melts. Add corn. Stir with wooden spoon to keep from sticking. Rinse grater over bowl, using about ½ to ¾ cup water. Add to corn in skillet. Season to taste. Cook over low heat, stirring often to avoid sticking, for about 40 minutes. Add more water, if necessary.

L. Randall 'Randy' Finfrock for his aunt
Celia Ann Massingill, Enterprise

Corn Casserole

1 (8-ounce) package cream
   cheese, softened
2 cans whole-kernel corn, drained
1 cup shredded cheese
1 can fried onions
1 stick butter, melted

Spread cream cheese in bottom of a 1-quart baking dish. Pour corn over cream cheese. Top with cheese then onions. Pour melted butter over top and bake at 350° until brown.

Leanne Townsend, Lena

Shoe Peg Corn Custard

2 (3-ounce) packages cream cheese
¼ cup milk
3 tablespoons butter
Dash garlic salt
2 cans white shoe peg corn, drained
Cheddar cheese, grated
1 (4-ounce) can chopped green chilies

Melt cream cheese with milk and butter in small heavy-bottomed saucepan. Add garlic salt and corn. Pour into a 9x13-inch casserole dish treated with butter. Top generously with cheese. Place green chilies at close intervals amid the cheese. Bake at 350° for about 30 minutes.

L. Randall "Randy" Finfrock and his mother
Lois Virginia Finfrock, Enterprise

Red Beans with Rice

1 (3½-ounce) bag boil-in-bag
   long-grain rice
4 ounces andouille sausage, diced
1 cup chopped red bell pepper
1 cup chopped onion
1½ to 2 teaspoons Cajun seasoning
1 teaspoon dried thyme
½ teaspoon hot pepper sauce
1 (16-ounce) can dark kidney beans, rinsed and drained
1 (14-ounce) can chicken broth
¼ cup chopped fresh parsley
½ teaspoon salt

Cook rice according to package directions. Heat a large nonstick skillet over medium-high heat. Coat pan with cooking spray. Add sausage; cook 3 minutes or until lightly browned. Using a slotted spoon, transfer sausage to a bowl, and keep warm. Add bell pepper, onion, Cajun seasoning, thyme and hot pepper sauce to pan; sauté 3 minutes or until onions are tender. Add beans and broth; cook 8 minutes or until thick, mashing half the beans. Add sausage, parsley and salt to pan; cook 1 minute or until thoroughly heated, stirring occasionally. Serve over rice. Serves 4.

The Murray's Mississippi Creole Rice

1 beef bouillon cube
1 pound ground beef
2 small onions, chopped
1 red bell pepper, chopped
½ cup chopped celery
Butter
1 can diced tomatoes
2 cups cooked rice
Salt and pepper
2 tablespoons Cajun seasoning
Grated cheese if desired

This easy recipe is one given to my grandmother, Harriet Whitaker, by her neighbor Francis Murray. The Murray's lived behind Gramp and Granny and according to my dad were quite good at playing the game Canasta.

Dissolve beef bouillon cube in ½ cup hot water. Brown beef; drain and set aside. Brown onions, bell pepper and celery in some butter. Combine bouillon, beef, cooked vegetables and remaining ingredients in a greased glass baking dish. Bake at 350º for 30 to 45 minutes. Do not dry out. Top with cheese, if desired.

Francis Murray
from the kitchen of
Harriett Whitaker, Grenada

Cheesy Rice Bake

2 tablespoons butter/margarine
1 bunch green onions, finely chopped
3 cups cooked long grain rice
2 cups grated sharp Cheddar cheese
1 (5-ounce) can evaporated milk
1 (4-ounce) can sliced mushrooms, drained
⅛ teaspoon Tabasco
1 tablespoon Worcestershire sauce
1 teaspoon dry mustard
½ teaspoon salt
⅛ teaspoon pepper
1 (10¾-ounce) can cream of celery soup

Preheat oven to 350°. In small saucepan, gently melt butter/margarine. Add green onions and simmer until softened. In a 1-quart casserole, combine all ingredients. Cook 30 to 35 minutes. Microwave: Use FULL power. In a 1-quart microwave casserole, melt butter for 45 seconds. Add onion; stir and cook 3 to 4 minutes. Add remaining ingredients and stir well. Cook 5 to 6 minutes; let stand 1 to 2 minutes before serving. Serves 4 to 6.

Annie Lou Shaw

Mexican Macaroni & Cheese

2 (12-ounce) packages elbow macaroni
1 stick butter
2 (8-ounce) packages grated sharp Cheddar cheese, divided
1 (8-ounce) package grated Colby/Monterey Jack cheese
1 (32-ounce) bar Velveeta cheese, cubed
2 cans Rotel tomatoes (do not drain)
Milk
Jalapeño peppers (sliced)
1 (8-ounce) package grated mozzarella cheese

I usually take this to church gatherings and family reunions because it makes so much. It is a real hit with everyone; there are never any leftovers.

Cook macaroni according to package directions; drain. Add butter and 1 package Cheddar cheese; stir well. Add Colby/Monterey Jack cheese, Velveeta cheese, Rotel tomatoes and enough milk to make it soupy. If necessary, microwave to melt cheese. Add jalapeño peppers to taste (I use about 4 tablespoons). Pour into 2 (9x13-inch) baking dishes. Combine mozzarella cheese and remaining package Cheddar cheese; sprinkle on top. Put about 8 or 10 slices jalapeño peppers on top of each dish for decoration.

Rose Compere, Mendenhall

Macaroni Casserole

1 pound hamburger meat
1 (12-ounce) package elbow noodles
1 can whole-kernel corn
1 (16-ounce) block Velveeta cheese, cubed
Salt and pepper

Brown hamburger meat; drain. While meat is browning, boil noodles as directed; drain. Combine noodles, hamburger, corn and cheese in a large saucepan; stir well. Simmer until cheese has melted. Season to taste.

Tammy Peavy, Carthage

Green Bean & Broccoli Casserole

2 (9-ounce) packages frozen cut green beans
2 (9-ounce) packages frozen broccoli
1 (11-ounce) can Cheddar cheese soup
½ cup milk
½ cup mayonnaise
1 cup shredded Cheddar cheese

Preheat oven to 325°. Grease 8x12-inch baking dish. Cook green beans and broccoli according to package directions. Drain well and place in baking dish. In large bowl, combine soup, milk and mayonnaise. Pour over vegetables. Top with cheese. Bake 45 minutes.

Chelsea Westbrook, Brandon

Zesty Butter Beans

1 medium onion, chopped
¼ cup chopped bell pepper
1 clove garlic, minced
¼ cup margarine
1 (14½-ounce) can chopped tomatoes
1 (10-ounce) package frozen baby lima beans
½ cup shredded mozzarella cheese

Sauté onions, bell pepper and garlic in margarine; set aside. Drain tomatoes, reserving liquid. Simmer lima beans in tomato juice, adding water to cover, until almost tender; drain. Combine onion mixture, reserved tomatoes and beans in casserole. Bake, covered, at 350° for 20 minutes. Uncover, top with cheese, and return to oven just until cheese melts. Serves 4 to 6.

Aunt Zue's Butter Beans

3 to 4 slices bacon (for drippings)
1 quart frozen speckled butter beans
1 tablespoon butter
1 teaspoon sugar
Salt and pepper to taste
3 to 4 pods fresh okra (whole)

These beans, and a pan of cornbread, will take you right back to my Aunt Zue's porch!

Cook bacon crisp in a saucepan. Remove bacon to drain on paper towels; leaving drippings in the pan. Add beans and enough water to cover. (Can use dried beans is you soak first according to package directions.) Add butter, sugar, salt and pepper. Wash okra pods and drop into beans whole. Cook at high simmer for 40 to 50 minutes, adding more liquid if necessary. Adjust seasonings. Remove okra and serve on the side. You may crumble the bacon into the beans, but Aunt Zue usually did not. Cook 5 minutes more.

L. Randall 'Randy' Finfrock for his aunt
Zula May Brown, Enterprise

Cotton is King in Mississippi

© Javier Soto Vazquez • image from bigstockphoto.com

Delta Jubilee &
Best Burger in the Delta Cook-Off
June • Clarksdale

Mississippi's first state championship pork barbecue cooking contest was held in 1984 on a riverbank park in downtown Clarksdale. Associated with subsidiary events, these activities became known collectively as the Delta Jubilee. Delta Jubilee is a multi-faceted community event that includes a carnival, arts and crafts show, musical entertainment, and many other events. Each of these activities lasts for the duration of the event. Saturday events include a 5K run and walk, 10/25/50 mile bicycle ride, pet show, basketball shootout, "Best Burger in the Delta" Competition, gospel concert, 4H modeling, cheerleading competition, step show, children's fishing rodeo, frog jumping contest, softball tournament, and horseshoe pitching competition. Family-oriented activities are very important to Delta Jubilee. There is always wholesome musical entertainment, children's activities, good food and fun, and other activities for the entire family to be involved in. Delta Jubilee is sponsored by the Clarksdale/Coahoma County Chamber of Commerce.

662.627.7337 • clarksdale-ms.com

Baked Beans

1 pound ground beef
1 onion, chopped
2 cans Showboat Pork & Beans,
    drained and fat removed
¾ cup packed brown sugar
½ cup ketchup

Preheat oven to 350°. Brown ground beef and onion; drain off grease. Combine with beans, brown sugar and ketchup. Bake in a 9x13-inch casserole dish for 30 minutes.

Jennifer McMillon, Kosciusko

Slap Yo Mama Baked Beans

3 (8-ounce) cans pork and beans
1 to 2 pounds ground chuck
3 to 4 strips bacon
⅓ to ½ cup finely chopped onions
1 to 1½ cups brown sugar
    (use as little or as much as you like)
2 bottles brown sugar barbecue sauce

Mrs. Donna gave me this recipe a while ago and I started adding to it and making it for friends and family. It became a HUGE success and now I am known as the "Baked Bean Lady." Everyone calls to ask me to make this recipe for their event! Its all thanks to Mrs. Donna.

Preheat oven to 250°. Empty beans into a colander to drain. Wash until all juice has been removed and let sit in sink to dry. Brown ground chuck, drain and set aside. Fry bacon crisp; remove from pan reserving drippings. Chop bacon and set aside. Add chopped onions to bacon grease and cook until caramelized (browned). Pour beans into a large casserole dish spreading evenly. Add onions with grease, meat, bacon and barbecue sauce; mix well with a large spoon. Add brown sugar, reserving some for the top; stir. Lightly cover top with brown sugar. Bake 45 minutes to 1 hour. Do not stir; remove from oven and serve.

Donna Callendar Temple and Shannon Pace, Byram

Pineapple Casserole

1 stick butter, divided
1 (20-ounce) can crushed pineapple
¾ cup sugar
2 teaspoons flour
1 cup shredded cheese
2 tablespoons pineapple juice
1 sleeve Ritz crackers, crushed

Drain pineapple, reserving 2 tablespoons juice; set aside to continue draining. Grease baking dish with 2 tablespoons butter. Pour drained pineapple into dish. Combine sugar, flour and cheese. Pour over pineapple. Melt remaining butter; combine with crackers and reserved pineapple juice. Spread over top of casserole. Bake at 350° for 40 minutes.

Leanne Townsend, Lena

Cranberry Mold

1 pound fresh cranberries
2 cups sugar
3 (3-ounce) packages lemon gelatin
1 (4-ounce) can mandarin oranges, drained
1 (20-ounce) can crushed pineapple, drained
1 cup walnuts, whole or halves

Combine cranberries, sugar and 1 cup hot water in pot over high heat. Boil 15 minutes. Cranberries will pop like popcorn; stir frequently . Remove from heat. Add gelatin, orange slices, pineapple and walnuts. Pour into gelatin mold. Cool; then refrigerate. To remove from the mold, float mold in warm water for about 1 minute before inverting onto serving dish.

Valerie Mabry, Biloxi

Demaris Lee's Hot Fruit

1 (8-ounce) package dried apples
1 (8-ounce) package dried apricots
1 (8-ounce) package dried prunes
1 (20-ounce) can crushed pineapple (with liquid)
1 cup brown sugar
1 stick butter
Pecans

This is great for a brunch. I serve it to our Heritage Club ladies.

Mix all fruit; sprinkle brown sugar over all. Dot with butter; sprinkle with pecans. Cover and bake at 350° for 1 hour.

Demaris Lee, Petal

Beef & Pork

Barbecued Ribs page 129

Stuffed Bell Peppers

3 green bell peppers
1 pound hamburger meat
½ onion, chopped
Salt, pepper and garlic powder
1 can stewed tomatoes, chopped
¾ cup uncooked rice
¾ cup water
2 cups shredded Cheddar cheese

To prepare bell peppers, cut around top and remove stem portion and seeds. Rinse well inside and out. Place in a large saucepan with water to cover. Bring water to a boil and boil 3 to 4 minutes just until peppers are softened, not soggy. Remove from water immediately. While peppers are boiling, brown meat; drain. Add onion and continue to cook until onion is tender. Season to taste. Add tomatoes, rice and water; cook until rice is tender and water has been absorbed. Remove from heat and stir in cheese. Stuff meat mixture into peppers and bake at 350° about 30 minutes. Enjoy!

Melissa Slay, Brandon

Mexican Casserole

2 pounds hamburger meat
1 onion, chopped
1 family-size can cream of mushroom soup
8 flour tortillas, torn into pieces
2 cans diced Rotel tomatoes
1 can ranch-style beans
2 (8-ounce) packages shredded Cheddar cheese
1 (8-ounce) package shredded mozzarella cheese

This is my husband's favorite dish! He likes it served with corn casserole.

Brown hamburger meat with onions; drain and set aside. Layer ¼ soup then ¼ tortillas in bottom of a 2-quart glass casserole dish. Layer ½ meat and ⅓ cheese. Add a layer each ¼ soup and ¼ tortillas. Layer all beans and tomatoes then ⅓ cheese, ¼ soup and ¼ tortillas. Layer remaining meat, soup, tortillas then cheeses. Wrap in foil and bake at 425° for 35 minutes. Remove foil and bake an additional 15 minutes.

Teresa Vanlandingham, Brandon

Spanish Delight

1 large onion, chopped
1 large green bell pepper, chopped
½ cup oil
¾ pound ground beef
1 (17-ounce) can cream-style corn
1 can El Paso tomatoes and chilies (or Rotel)
1 (4-ounce) can chopped green chilies
1 can tomato paste
1 tablespoon chili sauce
1 teaspoon salt
1 teaspoon pepper
½ teaspoon hot sauce
1 (5-ounce) package egg noodles
2 cups shredded Cheddar cheese

Sauté onion and pepper in oil. Add beef and cook slowly until lightly browned. Add remaining ingredients, except noodles and cheese; simmer 20 minutes. Cook noodles according to package directions; drain and add to meat mixture. Pour into a lightly greased 2-quart casserole dish. Bake at 350º for 20 minutes. Remove from oven and sprinkle cheese on top and place back in oven until cheese is melted. Serves 8 to 10.

Stacy Jones, Louise

Sunset at the Beach
Biloxi

© Linda Bryan • image from istockphoto.com

Tater Tot Casserole

1 pound ground chuck
1 bag tater tots
1 can cream of mushroom soup
1 can cream of chicken soup
Salt and pepper
2 cups shredded cheese

Brown hamburger; drain and set aside. Lightly brown tater tots in skillet in a small amount of oil; drain. Layer ½ tater tots in bottom of 2-quart treated casserole dish. Combine meat, both soups, salt and pepper to taste. Pour over tater tots. Add a layer of remaining tater tots. Completely cover with cheese. Bake at 350° about 20 minutes or until hot and cheese has melted.

Krista Griffin, Carthage

The Slugburger Festival
2nd Weekend of July • Corinth

Every July, Corinth celebrates its very own gastronomic treat, the Slugburger. No, it's not a mollusk sandwich. It is actually a deep-fried burger made with pork, bread filler and secret spices served on a bun dressed with dill pickles, mustard and sweet onion. The Slugburger came about during the Depression when meat was scarce. Restaurants used filler to make the meat last longer. The burgers sold for a nickel, also known as a slug. Thus, the Slugburger was born. During the festival, folks can sample Slugburgers and come out on Thursday, Friday and Saturday evenings for musical entertainment and a carnival.

662.287.1550 • corinth.net

Talleronie Casserole

2 pounds ground beef
2 tablespoons shortening
3 garlic cloves, minced
2 onions, chopped
2 bell peppers, chopped
1 can tomato soup
1 can whole-kernel corn
1 (4.25-ounce) can chopped ripe (black) olives
1 (2-pound) package noodles,
**   prepared per package directions**
1 pound sharp cheddar cheese, shredded

Brown meat in skillet with shortening; drain. Add garlic, onion and bell pepper; continue to cook a few minutes, stirring constantly. Add soup, corn and olives. Cook until heated through; add a little water and stir often to keep from sticking. Layer ½ noodles in 9x13-inch casserole dish, cover with ½ meat mixture and ½ shredded cheese. Repeat layers. Place in oven at 350° and cook until cheese is melted and mixture bubbles.

Teresa Vanlandingham, Brandon

Mexican Corn Casserole

1 pound ground beef
1 large onion, chopped
Salt and pepper
1 can mexicorn
1 (8-ounce) package cream cheese
1 can cream of mushroom soup
1 to 2 cans refrigerated biscuits

Brown meat and onion; drain. Salt and pepper to taste. Add corn, cream cheese and soup. Pour into an 8x8-inch casserole dish and heat until bubbly. Top with biscuits, and cook until biscuits are done.

Rose Compere, Mendenhall

Betty's Easy Enchilada Pie

2 pounds hamburger meat
1 large onion, finely chopped or shredded
Salt and pepper
2 cans Rotel tomatoes
2 tablespoons chili powder
1 large package Dorito's (potato chips)
2 pounds Velveeta cheese

Sauté hamburger and onion; drain. Salt and pepper to taste. Add tomatoes and chili powder. Simmer 30 minutes. In large casserole dish, alternate layers of chips, meat mixture and cheese, ending with cheese. Bake at 350° for 30 minutes or until bubbly.

Jane Rather, Tupelo

Hamburger Casserole

2 pounds ground chuck
½ cup chopped bell pepper
½ cup chopped onions
1 (7.25-ounce) box macaroni & cheese
1 can whole-kernel corn
2 cans cream of mushroom soup
1 teaspoon Worcestershire sauce
1 teaspoon ketchup
Salt and pepper
2 cups shredded sharp Cheddar cheese

Preheat oven at 350°. Brown ground chuck with onions and bell pepper; drain. While meat is cooking, prepare macaroni & cheese per package directions. Combine meat mixture, macaroni & cheese, corn, soup, Worcestershire sauce and ketchup. Salt and pepper to taste, and pour into a casserole dish. Top with shredded cheese and bake until heated through and cheese has melted.

Kristy Lepard, Good Hope

Hamburger Potato Skillet

1 pound hamburger meat
1 teaspoon oil
1 onion, chopped
½ bell pepper, chopped
6 potatoes, peeled and chopped in ½-inch pieces
1 teaspoon salt
1 teaspoon pepper
1 teaspoon cayenne, optional

Brown hamburger meat; drain, removed from pan and set aside. Add oil, onions and peppers to pan and cook until soft. Add potatoes and slow fry until brown. Add hamburger and stir to combine. Add salt, pepper and cayenne; stir well. Simmer 20 minutes then serve. Optional: Top with ketchup, ranch dressing, or barbecue sauce.

Luann Richardson, Brandon

Dudies Burger Festival
First Saturday in May • Tupelo

Come relive the bygone days of carhops & 10 cent "Dough Burgers", hospitality style, in Tupelo, MS. The Oren Dunn City Museum, in conjunction with the "Blue Suede Cruise," recreates the nostalgia of Dudie's Diner, a 1947 Memphis Streetcar, made famous by its very own carhop & singer/songwriter, Gene Simmons, in the song, "Dudie's Diner." You will relive history while eating a Dudie Burger, made from the original recipe, in the vintage diner, now housed at the museum. Make this historic stop while Cruisin' through Tupelo!

662.841.6438 • tupelo.net

Dinner Special Meatloaf

1 pound ground chuck
½ cup original barbecue sauce
1 egg, lightly beaten
½ cup dry breadcrumbs
1¼ cups water
¾ cup milk
2 tablespoons butter
½ teaspoon salt
1½ cups instant potato flakes
3 ounces cream cheese, softened
2 cheese singles

Preheat oven to 375°. Mix meat, barbecue sauce, egg and breadcrumbs. Shape into a loaf in a 8x12-inch dish. Bake 55 minutes. Meanwhile, bring water to a boil in a medium saucepan; add milk, butter and salt. Stir in potato flakes. Stir in cream cheese until melted. When done, remove meatloaf from oven. Spread potato mixture over meatloaf. Top with cheese singles. Return to oven just until cheese is melted.

Leanne Townsend, Lena

Salsa Meatloaf

3 pounds ground beef
1 cup chopped onion
1 cup chopped bell pepper
1 jar salsa, divided
2 eggs, beaten
½ cup brown sugar
½ cup brown sugar
¼ cup Worcestershire sauce

Combine meat, onions, peppers, ½ jar salsa, eggs and Worcestershire sauce. Mold into a loaf. Place in baking dish. Combine remaining salsa, brown sugar and two splashes Worcestershire sauce. Pour over meatloaf. Bake at 350° for 60 minutes or until meat is done. Drain excess fat before serving.

Leanne Townsend, Lena

Mama Frock's Mississippi Meatloaf

1 pound ground chuck (or round)
¾ cup Stove Top Stuffing mix
3 tablespoons chopped onion
3 tablespoons chopped green bell pepper
2 to 3 tablespoons chopped celery
1 tablespoon chopped parsley
¼ cup grated Colby-Monterey Jack cheese
Milk
Ketchup

This recipe is from my mom Lois who learned to cook with her sisters and her mother. This is not just your average meatloaf, it's a true family favorite recipe!

Using hands, mix everything together, except milk and Ketchup. Add enough milk to moisten (so that mixture sticks together). Spoon into treated loaf pan (or be creative as occasion demands and form into shapes). Bake at 350° for 35 minutes. Drizzle ketchup over top and bake additional 5 to 10 minutes.

L. Randall 'Randy' Finfrock and his mother
Lois Virginia Finfrock, Enterprise

© Kent Whitaker

Beef Stroganoff

1 pound sirloin steak
1 can sliced mushrooms
½ cup minced onion
2 tablespoons butter
**1 (10½-ounce) can beef consommé,
    divided**
3 tablespoons flour
2 tablespoons ketchup
1 teaspoon salt
1 small clove garlic, minced
1 cup sour cream
Noodles or rice

*This was my grandfather's, Clyde Lee
Smith, recipe. I can remember standing
in a chair helping my grandparents cook,
and this was a favorite of mine.*

Cut meat into very thin slices then cube it. In a skillet over medium heat, cook and stir mushrooms and onions in butter until tender. Remove from skillet and set aside. In same skillet, brown meat lightly on both sides. Add ⅓ cup consommé, flour, ketchup and salt; stir well and continue to cook until heated through. Add remaining consommé, garlic and reserved mushrooms and onions. Heat until boiling; boil 1 minute. Stir in sour cream and heat thoroughly. Serve over noodles or rice.

Teresa Vanlandingham, Brandon

© Robyn Mackenzie • image from istockphoto.com

Beef Pot Pie

1 medium potato, chopped small
1 medium onion, chopped small
1½ cups leftover cooked roast beef
1 can cream of onion soup
2 cans mixed vegetables, drain 1 can
Salt and pepper
1 tube crescent rolls
1 tablespoon butter or margarine, melted

Boil onion and potato until tender, drain. Mix meat, soup and vegetables; salt and pepper to taste. Pour in a 2-quart baking dish. Use rolls for top crust. Brush with melted butter or spray with butter-flavored Pam. Bake at 400º for 30 minutes or until brown.

Mary Ransom, Aberdeen

Easy Beef Tips Over Rice

1 large package beef stew meat
1 envelope Lipton Onion Soup Mix
1 can cream of mushroom soup
1 can Sprite

Combine all ingredients in a crockpot. Cook on high 4 hours. Serve over rice.

Melissa Webb, Ludlow

Chef Jenard Wells Steak Fajitas

Steak:

1 pound flank steak (or skirt steak or shrimp)
Olive oil
1 large yellow onion, peeled and sliced with the grain (not against the grain as one would normally slice an onion - slice first in half, and then slice off sections a half-inch wide at widest point)
2 large bell peppers, stemmed, seeded, de-ribbed, sliced lengthwise in half-inch wide strips

Marinade:

Juice of 1 lime
2 tablespoons olive oil
2 cloves garlic, minced
½ teaspoon ground cumin
½ fresh jalapeño pepper, seeded, ribs removed, finely chopped
¼ cup chopped fresh cilantro, including stems

Fixings:

Shredded cheese
Salsa
Shredded iceberg lettuce
Sour cream
Guacamole
Warm flour tortillas

Mix all marinade ingredients. Add steak; marinate at least an hour (the longer the better). Heat a large cast iron pan or griddle to high heat; add a teaspoon olive oil. Add steak, frying on each side 3 minutes (medium rare) or longer. If pan smokes too much, reduce heat to medium-high. Remove steak from pan and let sit 5 minutes. Reduce heat to medium high, and add a little more oil to the pan if necessary. Add onions and bell peppers. Cook, stirring frequently, 5 minutes or until onions are slightly translucent. Slice meat against the grain into thin slices. (If you slice the meat at a slanted angle, you will be able to get your slices thin. Flank steak is flavorful but can be a little tough; thin slices will help make it easier to eat.) Serve immediately with shredded cheese, salsa, shredded iceberg lettuce, sour cream, guacamole and warm flour tortillas. (Hint for warming tortillas; put in microwave over a paper towel for 20 seconds on high heat.)

Chef Jenard Wells, originally from Michigan City, Mississippi

Grenada Mustard BBQ Sauce

1 cup mustard
½ cup ketchup
2 tablespoons honey
¼ cup hot sauce
¼ cup finely minced onion
Dash lemon juice
Splash cola

This is a family favorite that came to me from my grandfather and my dad, Eli and Eli III, both from Grenada. It is simple to make, but full of flavor.

Mix all ingredients together in a saucepan. Simmer until onions are soft. Remove from heat and thin with water, if needed. Delicious as a sauce or as a baste on all kinds of meat.

Grilling on the River
Second Weekend in April • Columbus

Grilling on the River is a free event held each year along the Columbus Riverwalk. It benefits the Columbus-Lowndes Humane Society. Everyone is sure to enjoy all the great food including competition barbeque samples prepared by the cook teams at the Food Giant "Peoples Choice" tent (you be the judge), plus hamburgers, hot dogs, philly cheesesteak, polish sausage, funnel cakes, lemonade, iced tea, and more from our food vendors. Join us Friday and Saturday for unique contests, a car and bike show, live music, craft vendors, and much more fun for the whole family.

662.328.6850 • grillingontheriver.8m.net

Granny's BBQ Sweet Sauce

1 medium onion, chopped
2 tablespoons oil or butter
2 tablespoons brown sugar
2 tablespoons vinegar
4 tablespoons lemon juice
1 cup ketchup
3 tablespoons Worcestershire sauce
½ tablespoon mustard
1 cup water
½ cup finely chopped celery
Large dash salt
Large dash red pepper flakes

This recipe is in my grandmother's handwritten cookbook. Seems she used a variety of sauces just like me. It must run in the family.

In a medium saucepan over medium heat, brown onion in olive oil or butter. Reduce heat to low and add remaining ingredients. Simmer until thick, about 30 minutes, stirring occasionally.

Harriett Whitaker, Grenada

© Jill Chen • image from istockphoto.com

Barbecued Ribs

6 pounds spareribs
 (pork ribs)
2 cups ketchup
½ cup fresh lemon juice
½ cup firmly packed brown sugar
1 tablespoon prepared mustard
½ cup finely chopped onion
¼ cup butter
¼ cup Worcestershire sauce
1 clove garlic, minced
⅛ teaspoon hot sauce

In a large pan, cook the ribs in boiling water 45 to 60 minutes or until tender. Remove ribs from pan and drain. Meanwhile, in a medium saucepan, combine all remaining ingredients. Simmer uncovered for 20 minutes, stirring occasionally. Place ribs on oiled grill over medium heat. Grill ribs as desired, turning and basting frequently with sauce. Refrigerate leftovers.

Harriet Whitaker, Grenada

Crockpot Pork BBQ

1 (5- to 6-pound) Boston butt
2 (12-ounce) bottles barbecue sauce, divided
1 large onion

Trim outside fat off pork butt. Put into crockpot that has been treated with nonstick spray. Add 1 bottle barbecue sauce. Cook 8 hours on low. Remove meat from pot; drain and cool. Cut in small pieces removing fat, gristle and bone. Clean pot and treat with nonstick spray. Return meat to pot; add onion and remaining bottle barbecue sauce. Cook on high 4 hours.

Mary Ransom, Aberdeen

Lorraine's French Meat Pie

2 onions
½ cup water
1 pound ground pork
½ teaspoon sage
½ teaspoon allspice
2 teaspoons salt
1 cup fresh breadcrumbs
1 small potato,
    boiled and chopped (optional)
2 frozen pie shells

In a food processor, grind onions while adding ½ cup water. Place in a pan over medium heat; and heat. Add pork, sage, allspice and salt. Cook until meat is browned. Taste and adjust spices as needed. Remove from heat, stir in breadcrumbs and potatoes; cool for a few minutes. Spoon into one pie shell and cover with other pie shell. Bake at 450° about 25 minutes.

Lorraine McCormick, Biloxi

Philadelphia Ham Jam Arts Festival
3rd Weekend in April • Philadelphia

The Philadelphia Ham Jam Arts Festival is a project of the Philadelphia Main Street Association. Held the third weekend of April each year, Ham Jam is our biggest promotional event. This year's event brought 15,000 people to the downtown area for the weekend. There's no better way to create energy and new life downtown than to throw a huge party! Over 200 Neshoba Countians are involved by volunteering, participating in the talent show or local entertainment, cooking in the barbecue contest, or taking part in the Hog Wild Run. There is also a huge kid's area for the young ones to enjoy!

601.656.1000 • hamjamartsfestival.com

Oven Fried Pork Chops

Pork Chops
Flour
Salt and Pepper
Oil

Flour and season chops. Place in 9x13-inch baking dish with 3 tablespoons oil. Arrange pork chops so that they are not touching. Cover with foil. Bake at 450° for 40 minutes. Turn chops. Bake another 30 minutes. Remove foil. Bake at 500° for 10 minutes. Remove from dish. Enjoy.

Mary L. Ransom, Aberdeen

Fran's Pork Florentine

1 (16-ounce) package frozen chopped spinach
1 (1½- to 2-pound) pork tenderloin
Salt and pepper
⅔ to 1 cup olive tapenade
½ to ¾ cup crumbled feta cheese

As a newlywed, I thrilled in the freedom of having my own kitchen. This is one of the first recipes I created, and I love that it adds a new twist to an old classic. Blue cheese and dried cranberries work well in place of the olives and feta.

Season and cook spinach per package directions; drain and squeeze dry. Preheat oven to 425°. Salt and pepper outside of tenderloin to taste. Using a very sharp knife, and being careful not to slice all the way through meat, make a long horizontal slice about ½ inch from bottom to about ½ inch from other side. Open up pork like a book, and make another incision, again toward bottom of meat ½ inch shy of opposing side. Press down to flatten. Lightly grease a roasting rack with cooking spray, and line the pan with aluminum foil. Set opened pork on top of roasting rack, perpendicular to the rings of the rack. Spread olive tapenade evenly on pork, pressing into meat. Spread spinach on top of tapenade, again pressing down to flatten. Top with feta cheese. Slowly roll up pork lengthwise, and tie with kitchen twine. Roast 30 to 45 minutes, or until internal temperature reaches 155° to 160°. Allow meat to rest 5 minutes after removing from oven.

Fran Stallings Peacock, Jackson

Sausage Boat

1 large loaf bread,
  unsliced
1 pound bulk pork sausage,
  cooked and drained
1 pound bacon
  (cooked, drained, and finely crumbled)
1 (8-ounce) package grated medium Cheddar cheese
1 (8-ounce) package grated Swiss cheese
1 large egg, beaten
1 tablespoon minced onion
2 tablespoons butter, melted
1 (12-ounce) can (1½ cups) evaporated milk
1 medium jar cherry preserves
Powdered sugar

Cover bottom and sides of bread with foil. Cut a large oval hole out of the top of the bread. Carefully scoop out inside, leaving sides strong and intact. Shred bread pieces in blender; place in large mixing bowl. Add next 8 ingredients; mix well. Spoon mixture into bread shell. Bake at 350° for 30 to 40 minutes. Remove from oven and cool 5 minutes. Remove foil, being careful not to break shell. Place on platter and spoon preserves on top. Sprinkle with powdered sugar. Slice and serve.

Ruth Grisham

Poultry

Stuffed Cabbage

1 large head cabbage
1 pound ground turkey
⅓ cup chopped onion
1 egg white
¼ teaspoon pepper
1 cup cooked rice

Boil cabbage until leaves are wilted; separate leaves. Mix remaining ingredients and mold into egg-size balls. Place each on a cabbage leaf, wrap and fasten with toothpicks. Brown lightly in a greased skillet. Cover and simmer 2 hours; add a small amount of water, if necessary. You may serve with tomato sauce or plain.

Chef Jenard Wells, The Love Chef,
originally from Michigan City, Mississippi

Drunk Chicken

1 (3-pound) chicken
Creole seasoning
Salt
1 (12-ounce) can beer
Picanté sauce
Worcestershire sauce

Preheat a charcoal grill to high heat. When coals are hot and glowing, carefully push them over to the sides of the grill, leaving an open space in the middle. Wash and drain chicken. Coat inside and out with Creole seasoning and a pinch of salt. Open can of beer and drink all but ⅓ of it. Add picanté sauce until almost full; add a splash of Worcestershire sauce. Place chicken over beer can, rear down so that can is inside the body cavity. Carefully place chicken in center of grill, facing 1 of the banks of coals (careful not to spill the beer). Cover grill and cook until chicken is tender and cooked through (1 to 2 hours).

Dayna Rose Johnson, Lena

Dixie Fried Chicken

1 fryer chicken, cut-up
2 eggs, beaten
1 teaspoon salt
½ teaspoon each black pepper
½ teaspoon paprika
½ teaspoon seasoned salt
2 tablespoons chopped parsley
½ cup all-purpose flour
2 cups Crisco

Wash chicken and set aside to dry. Combine eggs with seasoning. Coat each piece of chicken in egg mixture, then roll in flour. Fry chicken in large, heavy skillet over medium heat 15 minutes, turn and cook 10 minutes more or unil browned. Cooking time will depend on size of chicken. Cook chicken in batches ensuring that pieces do not touch. Turn chicken gently with tongs rather than a meat fork so chicken is not punctured and juices do not escape.

© Graça Victoria • image from bigstockphoto.com

Daddy's BBQ Southern Pecan Chicken

1 teaspoon vegetable oil
1 whole chicken, cut up
  (or about 4 pounds breasts and thighs, rinsed and patted dry)
1 tablespoon Daddy's BBQ™ Sweet Love™ Original Rub
2 small or 1 large onion, cut into wedges or thick rings
1 cup Lazy Magnolia's Southern Pecan Nut Brown Ale
1½ cups Daddy's BBQ Sauce

Heat oil in a large skillet over medium to high heat. Season chicken pieces with Daddy's BBQ™ Sweet Love™ Original Rub and brown chicken on both sides. Place in crockpot; add onions. Combine beer and barbecue sauce. Pour over chicken and onions. Cover and cook 3 to 4 hours on high heat or 7 to 8 hours on low.

Lazy Magnolia Brewing Co., Lee Hood, Kiln

D'Iberville BBQ Throwdown & Festival
Late February / Early March • D'Iberville

The D'Iberville BBQ Throwdown and Festival began just over a year after Hurricane Katrina devastated our small, growing city. City officials planned to hold an event that would take citizens' minds away from the continuing recovery and rebuilding and give them a fun-filled day of good music, family activities and great food. The first year saw 10 teams and 10 vendors. This past festival, we had 50 teams and 45 vendors. As our city grows by leaps and bounds, our little BBQ Throwdown is turning into a large event. We are now an official state-sanctioned event with over $5,000 in cash and prizes.

228.392.7966 • diberville.ms.us

Meema's Almond Chicken

6 boneless chicken breast halves
2 jars dried beef
6 to 8 slices bacon
1 (12-ounce) container sour cream
2 cans mushroom soup
1 package sliced almonds
1 cup grated medium Cheddar cheese

This recipe is hand-written from my grandmother's own family cookbook, and it is out of this world. It's very hearty and great for any time of year. My grandmother loved this recipe.

Wash chicken and pat dry with paper towels. Place beef slices in bottom of 9x12-inch baking dish overlapping slices as needed. Wrap chicken with bacon and place evenly over beef. In a bowl, mix sour cream and soup; spoon over chicken. Sprinkle with almonds and cheese. Bake at 250° for 4 hours (or at 350° for 3 hours). Makes a delicious gravy so serve with rice plus vegetables and a side salad.

John Stamoulis, in honor of his grandmother
Tina Kennedy, USCG Gulfport

"Less Fat" Fried Baked Chicken

6 skinless chicken breasts, halved
½ cup olive oil
½ cup flour
2 teaspoons dried tarragon
Fresh ground pepper

Rinse chicken breasts and set aside. Heat olive oil in skillet. Combine flour and tarragon. Sprinkle chicken with pepper then batter in flour. Brown on all sides about 10 minutes, remove from skillet, and place in baking pan. Bake at 350° for 45 minutes or until done. Remove from oven and serve.

Chef Jenard Wells, The Love Chef,
originally from Michigan City, Mississippi

Vicki's Easy Chicken Nuggets

1 package boneless skinless chicken strips
1 whole onion, sliced in wedges
2 eggs, beaten
Buttermilk
2 cups flour
¼ tablespoon seasoned salt
¼ teaspoon garlic powder
¼ teaspoon onion powder
Salt and pepper
Oil for frying

Slice chicken strips in half, long ways and place in a large bowl. Add onions and eggs. Add buttermilk to cover and refrigerate 2 to 24 hours. Combine flour with seasonings. Remove chicken from refrigerator; bring to room temperature. Heat oil for frying. For each strip, remove from marinade, allow to drip for a second, roll in seasoned flour, and deep fry until golden brown.

Vicki Lyn Thomas, Lena

© Joshua Resnick • image from bigstockphoto.com

Poppy Seed Chicken

1 sleeve Ritz crackers, crushed
2 tablespoons poppy seeds
1 stick butter, melted
4 chicken breasts, boiled and shredded
1 can cream of mushroom soup
1 can cream of chicken soup
1 (8-ounce) carton sour cream

Treat a 9x13-inch casserole dish with nonstick spray. Combine crackers, poppy seeds and butter. Sprinkle just enough to cover bottom of pan. Combine chicken, soups and sour cream. Spread over cracker layer. Top with remaining cracker mixture. Bake at 350° for 1 hour.

Vicki Thomas, Lena

Demaris Lee's King Ranch Chicken

4 to 5 boneless skinless chicken breasts
1 can cream of mushroom soup
1 can cream of chicken soup
½ can Rotel tomatoes
½ can chicken broth
1 dozen flour tortillas, torn in pieces
1 onion, chopped
2 to 3 cups grated cheese (How cheesy do you want it?)

Boil and debone chicken; cut into pieces. Layer ½ chicken in bottom of a 2½ quart greased casserole. Blend both soups, Rotel and chicken broth to make a sauce. Layer ½ tortilla pieces, ½ onion, ½ to 1 cup cheese and ½ sauce. Repeat layers. Finish with 1 cup cheese over top. Bake uncovered in 350° oven for 1 hour.

Demaris Lee, Petal

Baked Mushroom Chicken

4 boneless skinless chicken breasts, halved
Salt, pepper, onion powder,
**   Tony Chachere's or other seasonings**
8 slices bacon
8 slices Swiss cheese
1 can mushrooms
2 cans cream of chicken soup
Chives, optional

Rinse chicken breasts and pat dry. Season to taste. Wrap each half with bacon and Swiss cheese; hold it together with a toothpick. Pour mushrooms then soup over top. Sprinkle with chives, if desired. Bake at 375° about 1 hour or until chicken is done. Serve over rice. Yummy!

Lance Fletcher, Lena

Easy Chicken Enchiladas

4 to 5 boneless skinless chicken breasts
1 can diced green chilies
1 can cream of chicken soup
1 can cream of mushroom soup
1 package flour tortillas
2 cups shredded mozzarella cheese
2 cups shredded Cheddar cheese

Cook chicken (boil or bake, your preference); shred into a large bowl. Add green chilies, cream of chicken soup and ½ cream of mushroom soup. Mix well. Spoon mixture in middle of tortillas, top with cheese, fold, and lay face down in glass 9x13-inch pan. (You will use all of the chicken mixture and ⅔ of the cheese.) Pour remaining cream of mushroom soup over top. Sprinkle remaining cheese over top. Bake at 350° for about 30 minutes.

Amber Johnston, Lena

Cheesy Chicken Rolls

1 to 2 pounds chicken tenders,
    (boiled, and cooled and shredded)
1 can crescent rolls
1¼ cups milk
1 cup shredded cheese
1 can cream of chicken soup
1 teaspoon garlic powder

Divide chicken equally between crescent rolls, placing chicken along the largest part of the roll. Roll-up chicken in crescent rolls largest side to smallest tip. Place in a 9x13-inch baking dish. Combine milk, cheese and soup in a medium saucepan. Cook over medium heat until cheese is melted. Pour over rolls. Bake 40 minutes at 350° or until done.

Ellin Simmons, Lena

Wing Dang Doodle Festival
Last Saturday in September • Forest

Forest's Wing Dang Doodle Festival is a celebration of all things Mississippi, chicken and blues. With poultry being Mississippi's largest agricultural product (Scott County is the nation's fifth largest poultry producing county) and blues being one of the state's largest cultural products, the Forest Area Chamber of Commerce combined the two and created a spectacular festival. With over 30 cooking teams vying for the $1000 grand prize for the best wings around and the Blues entertainment as well as family activities, including a motorcycle blues run and 5K Run/Walk, the Wing Dang Doodle is a guaranteed crowd pleaser.

601.469.4332 • forestareachamber.com

Grilled Chicken Tacos

1 tablespoon vegetable oil
½ cup chopped onion
1 garlic clove, minced
2 cups cooked chicken
1 (14-ounce) package Azteca® flour tortillas
1½ cups shredded Monterey jack and Cheddar cheese
1 tablespoon margarine

Heat oil in skillet; cook onion and garlic until tender. Add chicken; heat 3 minutes. Remove from heat. Heat tortillas according to package directions. Divide chicken onto center of each tortilla. Top with cheese. Fold tortillas in half. Melt margarine in same skillet. Grill tacos 2 to 3 minutes on each side or until cheese melts.

Chelsea Westbrook, Brandon

Homemade Chicken Alfredo

1 pound chicken, cubed
Salt and pepper
3 tablespoons olive oil
1 large (16-ounce) package bow tie pasta
1 tablespoon minced garlic

Sauce:

1 pint half & half
1 pint sour cream
1 teaspoon pepper
2 teaspoons salt
½ cup Parmesan cheese

Bring all sauce ingredients to full rolling boil. Cover and simmer over very low heat for 10 minutes, stirring frequently. Rinse chicken and season with salt and pepper to taste. Sauté chicken in olive oil until done. Cook noodles per package directions adding 1 tablespoon minced garlic to the boiling water; drain. Combine chicken, sauce and noodles; serve.

Melissa Webb, Ludlow

Chicken Alfredo

2 boneless skinless chicken breasts
1½ teaspoons Watkins Original grapeseed oil
½ cup chopped red bell pepper
½ cup chopped yellow pepper
1 cup sliced mushrooms
¼ cup chopped green onion
½ cup Kalamata olives
1 pound pasta noodles
2 teaspoons all-purpose flour
¾ to 1 teaspoon Watkins garlic liquid spice
1 (12-ounce) can evaporated skim milk
½ cup grated Parmesan cheese
¼ teaspoon Watkins black pepper

Sauté chicken breast in grapeseed oil 6 to 8 minutes over medium heat. Add peppers, mushrooms and green onions. Continue cooking until vegetables are tender. Add olives. Meanwhile, cook your favorite pasta according to package directions. Remove chicken and vegetables from skillet; slice chicken. Brown flour in pan juices. Stir in garlic liquid spice and evaporated milk. Cook, stirring occasionally until thickened. Stir in Parmesan cheese. Coat cooked noodles with sauce; stir in vegetables and slices of chicken. Sprinkle with pepper.

Biloxi Shrimp Boats

Chicken Spaghetti

1 hen, cooked (reserve stock)
    and chopped
3 green bell peppers, chopped
3 large onions, chopped
1 (8-ounce) can mushrooms
Minced garlic to taste
1 can petits pois peas
    (very small green peas)
2 (16-ounce) cans tomatoes, mashed
2 cans tomato paste
1 can Campbell's® tomato soup
3 (10-ounce) packages spaghetti
Sugar
Salt
Worcestershire sauce
Tabasco
Black pepper
Red pepper
Mustard
1 pound cheese, chopped into small pieces

This recipe makes a bunch! If you aren't serving a crowd, eat some now and freeze the rest for later.

In a skillet over medium heat, combine ½ cup stock, peppers, onions, mushrooms (reserve liquid) and garlic; sauté. Combine chicken, pepper and onion mixture, mushroom liquid, peas with liquid, tomatoes, tomato paste and soup in large boiler or stockpot. Simmer 20 minutes or longer. Prepare spaghetti per package directions; drain. While spaghetti is cooking, add seasonings to taste and cheese to chicken mixture. Add cooked spaghetti, stir well, and simmer short time.

Annie Lou, Shaw

Easy Chicken Spaghetti

4 boneless skinless chicken breast
1 can Rotel
1 large package vermicelli pasta
1 (16-ounce) block Velveeta® cheese
1 can cream of mushroom soup
1 can cream of chicken soup
Salt and pepper to taste

Wash and cube chicken; brown chicken in skillet. Add Rotel and simmer while preparing noodles. Boil noodles as directed. Cube Velveeta and microwave until melted. Stir melted cheese and both soups into chicken; heat until hot. Drain noodles and add to chicken mixture; mix all well. Enjoy!

Mary Beemon, Good Hope

Delta Wings Festival
First Saturday in November • Drew

In March 2006, Drew became the "Waterfowl Capital of Mississippi". In conjunction with this designation, the Drew Chamber of Commerce and Mississippi Main Street decided to establish an annual festival to celebrate the abundant natural resources and wildlife in our area. The festival consists of vendors, children activities, local band, duck calling contest, duck gumbo cook-off, retriever shows, silent auction and much more.

662.745.8975 • deltawingsfestival.com

Creole Chicken and Vegetables

1 pound chicken breast tenders
2 cups frozen pepper stir-fry, thawed
1 cup frozen cut okra, thawed
¾ cup thinly sliced celery
¾ teaspoon sugar
½ teaspoon salt
½ teaspoon dried thyme
¼ teaspoon ground red pepper
1 (14.5-ounce) can diced tomatoes, undrained
¼ cup chopped fresh parsley
1 tablespoon butter

Heat a large nonstick skillet over medium-high heat. Coat pan with cooking spray. Add chicken; cook 3 minutes on each side or until browned. Add pepper stir-fry, okra, celery, sugar, salt, thyme and red pepper; stir. Pour tomatoes over chicken mixture; bring to a boil. Cover, reduce heat and simmer 5 minutes. Uncover; cook 3 minutes. Add parsley and butter, stirring until butter melts. Serves 4.

Huntington Chicken

1 cup chopped onion
1 stick butter
2 cups cooked and shredded chicken
1 (8-ounce) package egg noodles,
    prepared per package directions
1 can cream of celery soup
1 can cream of mushroom soup
1 small jar pimento
1 cup grated cheese

Cook onion in butter until tender. Combine with remaining ingredients using ½ cheese. Sprinkle remaining cheese over top. Bake at 350° until heated through and cheese and is melted.

Delma Frazier Rodabough, Amory/McCool

M.E.'s Chicken Spaghetti

3 cups cooked shredded chicken
Butter
2 small bell peppers, chopped
1 large onion, chopped
⅓ cup pimentos
1 can chicken broth
1 can chopped mushrooms
2 tablespoons Italian seasoning
1 can tomato sauce
1 tomato, chopped
Salt, pepper and garlic powder
1 (16-ounce) box spaghetti noodles
½ pound Velveeta cheese

Heat butter in skillet over medium heat; brown bell pepper and onion. Add pimentos, broth, mushrooms and Italian seasoning; heat. Add chicken and cook to reduce broth. Stir in tomato sauce and chopped tomato; simmer on low 15 minutes or longer. Add salt, pepper and garlic powder to taste. While sauce is simmering, prepare noodles per directions on box to al dente; drain. Before serving, stir cheese and noodles into sauce and heat just until cheese is melted and noodles are heated.

Harriett Whitaker, Grenada

Mama's Southern-Style Chicken 'N Dumplings

1½ cups flour
½ teaspoon salt
¾ teaspoon baking powder
1½ tablespoons butter
Milk
2 quarts chicken broth
2 to 3 cups cooked shredded chicken
Salt and pepper

Sift flour, salt and baking powder. Cut in butter. Add milk, 1 tablespoon at a time, to bring dough to consistency of pie dough. Roll dough out on floured board to ¼-inch thickness. Cut into strips. Cut strips into 2- to 3-inch lengths. Bring broth to rapid boil. Add chicken then salt and pepper to taste. Drop dumplings into boiling broth and cook until dumplings float to the top. Taste one to make sure they are no longer "doughy." You may add butter if you need more fat in the broth.

L. Randall 'Randy' Finfrock and his mother
Lois Virginia Finfrock, Enterprise

© Leslie Banks • image from istockphoto.com

Fish & Seafood

Spicy Asian Catfish with Stir Fried Vegetables page 153

Catfish Supreme

8 catfish fillets
Paprika
8 ounces tomato sauce
1 teaspoon lemon pepper seasoning
1 teaspoon garlic powder
1 teaspoon celery salt
1 tablespoon parsley flakes
Parmesan cheese

Sprinkle catfish fillets with paprika. Place fillets in glass baking dish. Mix tomato sauce and seasonings. Pour sauce over catfish, covering well. Cover with foil and bake at 350° for 20 minutes. Open foil, sprinkle with Parmesan cheese, replace foil and bake 5 more minutes. Uncover and run under broiler 2 to 3 minutes to brown cheese.

World Catfish Festival, Belzoni

Great Egret
Ocean Springs

© Ed Wenger • image from bigstockphoto.com

Catfish Parmesan

⅔ cup freshly grated Parmesan cheese
¼ cup all-purpose flour
½ teaspoon salt
¼ teaspoon pepper
1 teaspoon paprika
1 egg, beaten
¼ cup milk
5 to 6 small catfish fillets (about 2 pounds)
¼ cup (½ stick) margarine, melted
⅓ cup sliced almonds

Combine first 5 ingredients; mix well. Combine egg and milk; stir well. Dip fillets in egg mixture; dredge in flour mixture. Arrange in a lightly greased 9x13-inch baking dish; drizzle with butter. Sprinkle almonds over top. Bake at 350° for 35 to 40 minutes or until fish flakes easily when tested with a fork.

World Catfish Festival, Belzoni

Weight Watchers Catfish

½ tablespoon butter
1 onion, or to taste
4 catfish fillets
½ cup picanté sauce
2 slices mozzarella cheese

Slightly butter casserole dish. Slice onions in bottom and bake 15 minutes at 350°. Place 4 catfish fillets on onions; pour ½ cup picanté sauce on each fillet. Cover and bake 30 minutes. Uncover and place ½ slice Mozzarella cheese on each fillet. Broil until cheese melts.

World Catfish Festival, Belzoni

Catfish Lucie

4 catfish fillets
Salt and pepper to taste
1 to 2 lemons, to taste
Garlic powder, to taste
2 tablespoons white wine
Worcestershire sauce
4 strips bacon

Rub catfish fillets with salt and pepper then place in a shallow baking dish. Squeeze lemon juice over fillets. Sprinkle with garlic powder. Pour white wine over catfish; shake Worcestershire sauce to taste on fillets. Place strip of bacon on each fillet and cover with foil. Bake at 350° for 20 minutes. Uncover and bake 10 to 15 more minutes. Serve with green salad and baked potato.

World Catfish Festival, Belzoni

Horseradish Sauce

1 (8-ounce) carton sour cream
1½ tablespoons horseradish
1 teaspoon freshly squeezed lemon juice
1 teaspoon seasoned pepper

Combine all ingredients. Refrigerate until serving with freshly cooked catfish. This will keep at least a week in the refrigerator.

Catfish Women of the World

Spicy Asian Catfish with Stir Fried Vegetables

Asian Marinade:

6 ounces pear juice

¼ cup soy sauce

¼ cup rice vinegar

1 tablespoon grated fresh ginger

½ teaspoon ground red pepper

¼ cup honey

½ teaspoon ground mustard

Catfish:

3 to 4 U.S. farm-raised catfish fillets

3 teaspoons Chinese 5 spice

4 tablespoons olive oil

1 cup sliced mushrooms

1 cup snow peas

1 cup bias cut celery (thin)

1 cup sliced red and yellow bell peppers

1 cup bean sprouts

2 teaspoons cornstarch

½ teaspoon salt

Cooked rice or noodles for serving

In a medium bowl, whisk together marinade ingredients. Cut catfish into bite-size chunks. Place in a shallow dish and add Chinese 5 spice, tossing to coat. Add ½ cup marinade, toss to coat, and let sit 10 minutes. While fish is marinating, heat a large skillet or Wok over high heat for 2 minutes; add oil. Add all vegetables except bean sprouts; cook 3 minutes, stirring frequently. Remove with a slotted spoon and set aside. Add catfish to the hot skillet and stir fry 2 minutes. In a separate bowl, combine cornstarch and remaining marinade; stir until there are no lumps. Add to the pan with the catfish. Add vegetables and bean sprouts. Cook 2 minutes, or until sauce has thickened. Season with salt. Remove from heat; plate with your choice of rice or noodles.

The Catfish Institute, Jackson

Catfish Vermouth

1 tablespoon lemon pepper seasoning
3 to 4 U. S. farm-raised catfish fillets
¼ cup white vinegar
¼ cup dry vermouth

Sprinkle catfish fillets with lemon pepper seasoning and marinate white vinegar and vermouth for 1 hour. Simmer catfish 5 minutes on each side in a non-stick skillet until all the liquid is cooked out and the catfish is brown.

World Catfish Festival, Belzoni

Biloxi Seafood Festival
Second Weekend in September • Biloxi

Biloxi Seafood Festival is a celebration of family, community, and heritage. Enjoy seafood dishes, arts and crafts, and continuous live entertainment throughout the weekend. Entertainment will include Diki Du & the Zydeco Crew, Tim Gross and the Blue Blazes and more. Stop by the CYP Kids Village with inflatable slide and bungee obstacle, face painting and games. The Boys & Girls Club of the Gulf Coast will also host children's activities on Saturday. Enter the Sun Herald Annual Gumbo Championship Professional or Amateur competitions on Sunday for a chance to win awards, recognition in the Sun Herald, and bragging rights. The public is invited to enter the competition area and sample gumbo for a small additional fee. All proceeds will benefit the chamber's programs. For a complete list of rules and entry forms contact the Biloxi Chamber of Commerce.

228.604.0014 • biloxi.org

Smoked Catfish

**Mississippi-raised catfish fillets,
   as many as needed**
Creole seasoning, to taste

Cocktail Sauce:

1 cup ketchup
¼ cup freshly squeezed lemon juice
1 tablespoon horseradish
¼ teaspoon black pepper

Season catfish fillets with Creole seasoning. Cook on hot grill sprayed with nonstick cooking spray, until the fish are firm and flake easily with a fork. Combine cocktail sauce ingredients. Can be made ahead and refrigerated. Serve fish with cocktail sauce on the side.

World Catfish Festival, Belzoni

Catfish Amandine

2 tablespoons margarine, divided
1½ pounds U. S. farm-raised catfish fillets
¼ cup slivered almonds
1 teaspoon grated lemon zest
2 teaspoons lemon juice
Parsley sprigs and lemon wedges or slices for garnish

Melt 1 tablespoon margarine in a large skillet over medium heat. Add catfish fillets and cook 2 to 3 minutes each side or until fish flakes easily when tested with a fork. Transfer to serving platter and keep warm. In same skillet, melt remaining margarine. Add almonds, lemon zest and lemon juice; sauté 1 minute. Pour sauce over fillets and garnish with parley and lemon.

World Catfish Festival, Belzoni

Mississippi Cajun Catfish

4 U.S. farm-raised catfish fillets
½ cup fish breading
1 tablespoon Creole seasoning
1½ to 2 cups frying oil

Rinse catfish and set aside. Combine fish breading and Creole seasoning in a shallow bowl. Coat catfish in breading, lightly shaking off any excess. In a large skillet, heat oil over high heat. Fry catfish until golden brown, about 3 minutes per side. Place Cajun Catfish on a paper towel to drain. Serve immediately. Delicious served with Catfish Institute's Honey Dijon Bacon Potato Salad (page 74).

The Catfish Institute, Jackson

Stephanie's "Cock of the Walk" Fried Catfish

12 catfish fillets (4- to 5- ounces each)
2 eggs
½ cup milk
½ cup flour
1½ cups cornmeal
2 teaspoons salt
2 teaspoons seasoning salt
1 teaspoon black pepper
1 cup canola oil

Wash catfish fillets, cut them into serving-size pieces, and set aside. Whisk eggs and milk in a shallow bowl. Combine flour, cornmeal, salt, seasoning salt and pepper in a Ziplock bag. Dip each fillet in egg mixture, then drop in bag to coat with cornmeal mixture. Heat oil over medium-high heat to 375° in a large skillet. Fry coated catfish pieces 3 or 4 (don't crowd in pan) at a time, until golden brown on each side. Drain on paper towels.

Tartar Sauce:

1 cup mayonnaise
⅓ cup sweet relish
2 tablespoons lemon juice
1 tablespoon ketchup

Combine and serve with catfish. Keep refrigerated when not serving.

Stephanie Jackson, Faulkner

© Kimberly Johnson • image from bigstockphoto.com

Freshwater Prawn Quesadillas & Chipotle Sauce

Chipotle Sauce:

1 cup sour cream
¼ cup chipotle in adobo sauce, pureed

Quesadillas:

2 pounds U. S. farm-raised freshwater prawns, peeled
3 cups (packed) grated pepper jack cheese
1½ cups cooked and finely chopped bacon
3 cups shredded spinach, washed and spun dry
12 (8-inch) flour tortillas
¼ cup vegetable oil, as needed
Cilantro sprigs and lime wedges for garnish

A great recipe from Dolores & Steve Fratesi that combines the great flavor of their freshwater prawns with a very tasty Tex-Mex feel. The spinach adds color, texture and flavor and really makes the dish exciting.

Mix sour cream and chipotle in adobo sauce; stir in water. Pour into squirt bottle. Refrigerate until quesadillas are ready. For quesadillas, bring about 8 cups water to a boil; add 1 to 2 tablespoons salt, according to taste. Add prawns and cook about 3 minutes (be very careful not to over-cook). Drain and immediately immerse in ice water to stop cooking. Drain and chop chilled prawns into bite-sized pieces. Combine prawns, pepper jack cheese, bacon and spinach. Divide the mixture evenly on the tortillas. Fold tortilla in half and press down to flatten. Over medium heat in a large skillet or on flat top (we use the electric skillet which holds 4 tortillas at a time heated to about 250°), heat 1 teaspoon or so of oil. Cook quesadillas on both sides until cheese melts and tortillas are golden brown, about 1½ to 2 minutes per side. Add additional oil as needed. Cut quesadillas in half. Drizzle with Chipotle Sauce. Garnish with cilantro sprigs and serve with lime wedges. 12 servings.

Note: Chipotle in adobo sauce can be found canned where the Mexican foods are located in your grocery store.

Dolores & Steve Fratesi, Lauren Farms, Leland

Gwyn's Shrimp Dip

2 tablespoons oil

1 cup mayonnaise

¼ cup ketchup

2 tablespoons mustard

2 tablespoons Worcestershire sauce

2 tablespoons water

1 tablespoon garlic powder

1 onion, grated

Salt to taste

Lots of pepper

Combine all ingredients and serve with boiled shrimp or fried fish.

Gwyn Taylor, Morton

My late wife, Gwyn, made this dip for our family and friends to eat with Bass we filleted, cut in pieces the size of your thumb, and boiled in shrimp boil for 24 minutes. It was enjoyed by all!

St. Paul Seafood Festival
June • Pass Christian

The St. Paul Seafood Festival is an annual celebration held on Beachfront Scenic Street in Pass Christian. Indulge in delicious seafood including fried catfish, shrimp & oyster plate or poboy, seafood gumbo, egg rolls & kabobs, boiled crawfish, crab stuffed potatoes, hamburgers & hot dogs, funnel cakes and more. It is an event the whole family can enjoy with live music, carnival rides, arts and crafts, and a 5k run. In 1992, the event received national attention by being listed in The World Book Encyclopedia. Have fun and support St. Paul Catholic Elementary School.

228.596.1896 • seafood.passchristian.net

© Darryl Brooks • image from bigstockphoto.com

Cynthia and Larry's Marinated Shrimp

2 cups red wine vinegar
1 lemon, sliced
2 fresh jalapeño peppers (seeded,
   deveined, and finely minced)
3 cloves garlic, minced
4 tablespoons dried minced onion flakes
¾ cup super-fine sugar
4 pounds cooked shrimp, peeled
   and deveined (optional)
¼ cup fresh chopped cilantro
3 to 4 tablespoons capers
Salt and pepper to taste
1 teaspoon cayenne pepper (optional)

This recipe is from my good friends Cynthia & Larry. It is the best marinated shrimp I've eaten. It was delicious on Friday evening, but it was stupendous at the tailgate prior to the game the next day.

Pour vinegar into a pot over high heat. Stir in lemon slices, jalapeño peppers, garlic, onion flakes and sugar. Bring to rapid boil, stirring until sugar is dissolved. Remove from heat and cool to lukewarm. (I'm thinking this marinade would be good over many other foods beside shrimp.) Place shrimp, cilantro and capers in a resealable plastic bag. Pour lukewarm sauce into bag and seal; refrigerate over night, turning the bag several times. Before serving, remove shrimp from bag and drain liquid over the top. Season with salt, pepper and cayenne; toss well.

Emily Jones, Starkville

Meema's Shrimp Thermidor

1 cup chopped celery
½ cup chopped bell pepper
1 small can button mushrooms
1 small can mushrooms bits and pieces
1 stick butter or margarine
4 tablespoons flour
3 cups milk
3 cups cooked shrimp, peeled and deveined
Salt and pepper
1 cup grated medium Cheddar cheese

In a skillet over medium-high heat, sauté celery, bell pepper and both cans mushrooms in butter. Add flour and blend well. Add milk slowly while stirring to thicken. Add shrimp, salt and pepper to taste. Pour in 9x13-inch baking dish, cover with cheese and bake at 375° for 15 minutes. Serve with rice.

John Stamoulis, in honor of his grandmother, Tina Kennedy, USCG Gulfport

Belinda's Biloxi Shrimp Cheese Grits

1½ cups grits
4½ cups water
1 teaspoon salt
⅔ cup shredded cheese
½ stick butter
2 eggs, beaten
¼ cup milk
Salt and pepper to taste
1 cup salad shrimp
3 tablespoons real bacon bits
1 can green chilies, drained
Hot sauce to taste, optional

Cook grits in water with salt added. After grits are cooked, add cheese, butter, eggs, milk and salt and pepper to taste. Put in a casserole dish and stir in shrimp, bacon bits, green chilies and hot sauce (if desired). Bake 35 to 45 minutes, or until set, at 350°.

Belinda Johnston & Family, raised in Biloxi

Mississippi Gulf Shrimp and Eggplant Casserole

1 pound Mississippi Gulf Shrimp,
cleaned and peeled
4 cups peeled and cubed eggplant
1 cup diced green bell pepper
1 cup diced onion
1 cup diced celery
2 cloves garlic, crushed
2 tablespoons butter
2 cups cooked rice
1 tablespoon Worcestershire sauce
2 teaspoons salt
½ teaspoon black pepper
½ teaspoon thyme
¾ cup mayonnaise
1 cup breadcrumbs

Sauté eggplant, bell pepper, onion, celery and garlic in butter until vegetables are soft. Add remaining ingredients, except breadcrumbs, and mix well. Place in a 2-quart casserole dish. Spread breadcrumbs over top. Bake in preheated oven at 350° for 45 minutes.

Jan Boyd, Mississippi Department of Marine Resources

Crawfish Etouffée

1 stick butter
1 pound crawfish tails
1 medium onion, chopped
2 ribs celery, chopped
1 bell pepper, chopped
1 tablespoon paprika
1 teaspoon pepper
1 bay leaf
1 cup chicken broth

Melt butter in deep heavy frying pan. (Do not use cast iron skillet; it will discolor the crawfish.) Add crawfish and cook 2 to 3 minutes. Remove with slotted spoon and set aside. Add onion, celery, bell pepper and seasonings. Sauté 10 minutes, removing bay leaf after 5 minutes. Return crawfish to pan and add chicken broth. Stir and cook slowly, covered, for about 40 minutes. Serve over rice. Serves 4. May be frozen.

Teresa Vanlandingham, Brandon

Creole Crawfish Festival
Mid-April • Southaven

Mississippi will meet Louisiana with blues, Cajun and zydeco music. Festival offers fresh boiled crawfish, gumbo cooking competition, art vendors, Cajun puppet show, zydeco dance contest, silent auction, Kidz Art Exhibit, and much more. Festival benefits 'No Music Left Behind', which encourages residents to donate used band instruments. Working with high school band directors, recycled band instruments are donated to deserving students and schools in North Mississippi.

901.619.5865 • creolecrawfishfestival.com

© Terry Poche • image from shutterstock.com

Crabmeat Quiche

½ cup mayonnaise
2 tablespoons flour
2 eggs, beaten
½ cup milk
1 teaspoon Zatarain's seasoning
1 cup crabmeat
8 ounces grated Swiss cheese
½ cup chopped green onions
1 (9-inch) pie shell, unbaked

Mix mayonnaise, flour, eggs, milk and seasoning until well blended. Stir in crabmeat, cheese and green onions. Pour into shell and bake in 350º oven for 40 to 45 minutes or until set. Baked quiche may be served immediately or sliced and frozen. Microwave each individual frozen slice about 20 to 30 seconds.

Valerie Mabry, Biloxi

Tuna Burgers

2 eggs, beaten
2 cans tuna, drained
¼ cup chopped onion (or to taste)
2 tablespoons chopped celery (or to taste)
1 tablespoon pimento (or to taste)
¼ teaspoon garlic powder (or to taste)
Black pepper and salt
¼ cup breadcrumbs (more or less to make patties)
Olive oil
4 to 6 cheese slices

Combine all ingredients, except oil and cheese. Press into 4 to 6 patties. Brown patties in olive oil. Finish cooking in 350º oven for 10 minutes or until done. Melt slices of cheese on top and serve on buns!

Kate Rather, Tupelo

Cookies & Candies

Chocolate Crinkle Cookies page 167

Stephanie's Mississippi Mud Cookies

1 cup semisweet chocolate morsels
½ cup margarine, softened
1½ cups sugar
2 large eggs
1 teaspoon Watkins vanilla
1½ cups all-purpose flour
1 teaspoon baking powder
½ teaspoon salt
1 cup chopped mixed pecans and walnuts
½ cup Nestle or Hershey milk chocolate morsels
1½ cups (approximate) miniature marshmallows

Melt semisweet chocolate morsels in a small microwave-safe glass bowl at HIGH 1 minute or until smooth, stirring every 30 seconds. Beat margarine and sugar on medium speed until creamy; add eggs, 1 at a time, beating well after each. Add Watkins vanilla and melted chocolate. In a separate bowl, combine flour, baking powder and salt; gradually add to chocolate mixture, beating until well blended. Stir in nuts and milk chocolate morsels. Drop dough by heaping tablespoonfuls onto parchment paper-lined baking sheets. Press 3 marshmallows into top of each cookie. Bake at 350° for 10 to 12 minutes or until set. Remove to wire racks. Makes about 3 dozen cookies.

Stephanie Jackson, Faulkner

Windsor Ruins
Near Port Gibson

© Robert Lutrick • image from bigstock.com

Chocolate Crinkle Cookies

½ cup vegetable oil
4 ounces unsweetened chocolate, melted
2 cups sugar
4 eggs
2 teaspoons vanilla
2 cups flour
2 teaspoons baking powder
½ teaspoon salt
1 cup powdered sugar

Combine oil, melted chocolate and sugar. Add eggs, mixing well after each. Add vanilla; stir in flour, baking power and salt. Chill overnight. Preheat oven to 350°. Drop dough by teaspoonful into powdered sugar and coat lightly. Roll into a ball then coat again in powdered sugar. Place 2 inches apart on greased baking sheets. Bake 10 to 12 minutes. Do not overcook. Makes about 4 dozen small cookies.

Mary Alice Bookhart's Creole Lace Cookies

1 cup Quaker Quick Oats
3 tablespoons flour
1 cup sugar
½ teaspoon baking powder
1 teaspoon salt
1 stick butter
1 teaspoon vanilla
1 egg, beaten
1 cup finely chopped toasted pecans

Combine oats, flour, sugar, baking powder and salt. Cut in butter. Add vanilla and egg; mix well. Refrigerate overnight. Drop marble-size portions (I use the small end of melon-baller dipped in water) 3 inches apart on cookie sheet lined with parchment paper. Bake at 325° for about 11 minutes. Cool on parchment. (I use 2 to 3 pieces of parchment so I can keep moving.) Store in airtight container.

Harry Baldwin, Canton

Sugar Cookies

1 egg
½ cup shortening
1 cup sugar
1 teaspoon vanilla
2 tablespoons milk
2 cups flour

Preheat oven to 400°. Mix all ingredients in bowl and knead. Roll on waxed paper to ¹/₆-inch thick. Cut with cookie cutter shapes or a small round glass dipped in sugar. Sprinkle with sugar then place on treated cookie sheet. Bake 5 to 7 minutes.

Alice Henderson, Florence

Cream Cheese Sugar Cookies

1 (8-ounce) package cream cheese, softened
1 cup powdered sugar
¾ cup butter, softened
1 teaspoon vanilla
2 cups flour
½ teaspoon baking soda

Beat cream cheese, both sugars, butter and vanilla with electric mixer on medium speed. Add flour and baking soda; mix well. Refrigerate several hours or overnight. Shape dough into 2 equal pieces. Roll dough to ¼-inch thickness on lightly floured surface. Cut into shapes using cookie cutters and place on ungreased baking sheet. Bake at 350° for 8 to 10 minutes or until edges are lightly browned. Cool 2 minutes then transfer to cooling racks.

Leanne Townsend, Lena

Gingersnaps

¾ **cup oil**
1¼ **cups sugar, divided**
1 **egg, beaten**
4 **tablespoons molasses**
2 **cups all-purpose flour**
½ **teaspoon salt**
1 **teaspoon cinnamon**
2 **teaspoons baking soda**
1 **teaspoon ginger**

Mix oil and 1 cup sugar. Add egg; mix. Stir in molasses. Sift flour, salt, cinnamon, baking soda and ginger. Add to molasses mixture; beat well. Roll into teaspoon-sized balls. Roll in remaining ¼ cup sugar. Place on lightly greased cookie sheet. Flatten with a fork; turn fork and press again to create a cross pattern. Bake 15 minutes at 350° until brown.

© Sally Scott • image from bigstockphoto.com

Stephanie's Cinnamon & Spice Cookies

2 cups all-purpose flour
1½ teaspoons baking soda
1 teaspoon purest ground cinnamon
6 ounces organic nutmeg
½ teaspoon salt
1½ cups sugar, divided
12 tablespoons butter (1½ sticks), softened
1 egg
½ teaspoon original double-strength vanilla
¼ cup molasses

Preheat oven to 350°. In a medium bowl, combine flour, baking soda, cinnamon, nutmeg and salt. With an electric mixer, beat 1 cup sugar, butter, egg, vanilla and molasses until well blended. Combine with dry ingredients until dough forms. Roll dough into 1-inch balls and dip in ½ cup reserved sugar. Arrange on a baking sheet about 3-inches apart. Bake 10 to 15 minutes. Makes 3 dozen. Enjoy.

Stephanie Jackson, Faulkner

Praline Cookies

24 graham crackers
1 cup packed brown sugar
1 cup butter
1 teaspoon vanilla
1 cup chopped pecans

Break graham crackers where marked and place them close together in the bottom of a jelly-roll pan. Bring brown sugar and butter to a boil; boil 2 minutes, stirring constantly. Remove from heat; stir in vanilla and nuts. Pour over crackers and bake 10 minutes at 350°. Cool slightly and cut into bars. Cool thoroughly and store in airtight container.

Tea Cakes

½ cup butter or
    margarine, softened
1 cup sugar
1 egg
2 tablespoons ice water
1 teaspoon vanilla extract
1¼ cups all-purpose flour
1 teaspoon cream of tartar
   (very important)
½ teaspoon baking soda
¼ teaspoon salt

Cream butter and sugar. Add egg, water and vanilla. Combine dry ingredients and gradually add to butter mixture. Chill thoroughly. Roll very thin on lightly floured surface. Cut with a round cookie cutter or glass dipped in flour. Bake at 350° about 8 minutes or until brown.

Hog Wild Festival
First Weekend in October • Corinth

Go Hog Wild in Corinth on the first weekend of October. A Kansas-city sanctioned event, Hog Wild features nightly entertainment and a carnival Thursday through Saturday. On Saturday, Hog Wild features a Back Yard Barbecue contest where locals cook and the public can sample and vote for the best barbeque.

662.287.1550 • hogwildfestival.com

© Malino • image from bigstockimage.com

Fruit Cake Cookies

3 cups sifted flour
1 teaspoon baking soda
½ teaspoon salt
2 teaspoons cinnamon
½ teaspoon cloves
½ teaspoon allspice
2 sticks (1 cup) butter, softened
1 cup packed light brown sugar
3 eggs
½ cup buttermilk
6 cups chopped nuts
1 pound red candied cherries, chopped and floured
1 pound green candied cherries, chopped and floured
½ pound candied pineapple, chopped and floured
2 cups dates (or raisins)

After sifting and measuring flour, sift again with baking soda, salt, cinnamon, cloves, and allspice; set aside. Cream butter and sugar; beat in eggs. Add flour mixture and buttermilk; mix well. Stir in remaining ingredients and mix thoroughly (dough will be stiff). Drop from teaspoon onto treated cookie sheets. Bake at 325° for 20 to 25 minutes. Makes about 8 dozen.

Gene's Lemon Cookies

½ cup milk
1 packet Dream whip mix
1 box lemon cake mix
1 egg
Powdered sugar

Preheat oven to 350°. Combine Dream Whip and milk. Add cake mix and egg; blend well. Roll dough into 1 inch balls. Dip balls into powdered sugar. Spray cookie sheet with Pam. Space out balls on cookie sheet (do not flatten). Bake about 8 minutes, cooking time may vary. Do not allow tops to brown, cookies should be extra moist.

The Little Family, Brandon

Bald Cypress Swamp

© Royce Bair • image from bigstockphoto.com

Chess Squares

Crust:

1 yellow or lemon cake mix
1 egg
½ cup melted margarine

Mix together and pat in a greased 9x13-inch pan.

Filling:

1 (8-ounce) package cream cheese, softened
3 eggs
1 (16-ounce) box powdered sugar
1 teaspoon vanilla

Mix well and pour onto crust mixture. Bake at 375° for 30 to 40 minutes. Cook and cut into squares.

Delma Frazier Rodabough, Amory/McCool

Rich, Chocolate Brownies

Brownies:

1½ cups all-purpose flour
1 teaspoon salt
½ cup plus 2 tablespoons cocoa
2 cups sugar
1 stick butter, softened
½ cup Crisco shortening
4 eggs
1 cup whole pecans, toasted
2 teaspoons vanilla

Frosting:

1 stick butter, softened
6 tablespoons cocoa
1 pound powdered sugar
1 teaspoon vanilla
⅓ cup half and half

This recipe has been a favorite of my family for over 20 years. It is chewy and loaded with chocolate. The frosting on top and the toasted pecans make these brownies decadent. We won't use any other brownie recipe in my family, because this one can't be beat!

Place brownie ingredients in mixing bowl. Beat at medium speed 3 minutes. Pour in greased 9x13-inch pan. Bake at 350 º for 30 minutes; cool while mixing frosting. Blend all frosting ingredients until smooth. (You may half this recipe if you want a thin layer of frosting.) Spread over brownies while slightly warm.

Pam Simpson, Vancleave, MS

Mint Chocolate Bars

3 sticks margarine, divided
½ cup cocoa
3½ cups powdered sugar, divided
2 cups crushed graham crackers
⅓ cup creme de menthe
1 (12-ounce) package chocolate chips

Melt 1 stick margarine in saucepan. Stir in cocoa, ½ cup powdered sugar and graham cracker crumbs. Press into bottom of 9x13-inch pan. Melt 1 stick butter in mixing bowl. Add creme de menthe and 3 cups powdered sugar. Mix on high speed until thoroughly combined. Pour over crust; chill 1 hour. Melt 1 stick margarine in saucepan over medium heat and stir in chocolate chips until melted. Spread over mint layer. Chill at least 1 hour. Cut into small squares before serving. Keep refrigerated.

Desoto Shrine Club BBQ Festival
June • Hernando

The Desoto Shrine Club BBQ Cook Off "SHRINEFEST" is held at the Desoto Shrine Club facility located on 53 acres at 2888 Gwynn road in Hernando. We are a Kansas City Barbecue Society Sanctioned event and host in excess of 50 teams, all reaching for their share of a $7200 purse. A Bike Fest is sponsored by the Knights of the South Widows Sons Masonic Motorcycle Riding Association. You will also enjoy a car show by the Sugar Ditch Cruizers car club. An open air lawnchair concert with 5 bands playing on Friday and Saturday ends Saturday night with our headliner, "Dirt Brothers". Join us for good fun for the whole family

662.890.3430 • desotobbq.com

Easy Shortbread Squares

1 cup butter, softened
2 cups all-purpose flour
½ cup powdered sugar
Dash salt

Preheat oven to 325°. Cream butter; add flour and sugar and mix into soft dough. Press into a 9-inch square pan. Bake 20 to 25 minutes. Cut into squares before shortbread cools.

Bessie Jackson, from the kitchen of
Harriett Whitaker, Grenada

Peanut Butter Bars

1 cup all-purpose flour
½ cup packed brown sugar
½ teaspoon soda
½ teaspoon salt
½ cup (1 stick) butter, softened
⅓ cup crunchy peanut butter
1 egg
1 cup uncooked oatmeal
1 (12-ounce) package white chocolate chips

Topping:

½ cup sifted powdered sugar
½ cup crunchy peanut butter
2 to 4 tablespoons milk

Mix flour, sugar, baking soda, salt, butter, peanut butter, egg and oats. Press dough into greased 9x13-inch pan. Bake at 350° for 20 minutes. Remove and top with chocolate chips. Let stand 5 minutes or until melted; spread evenly. Combine topping ingredients; beat well. Pour over top. Cut into bars.

Harriett's Chocolate Sweet Peanuts

2 blocks candy chocolate,
  white or brown
2 cups honey roasted peanuts
1 cup peanuts
Coconut flakes, optional

Melt chocolate per package directions. Combine peanuts and coconut (if desired). Add to melted chocolate; mix well. Drop by small spoonfuls onto waxed paper and cool.

Harriett Whitaker, Grenada

Cornflake Candy

1 cup white corn syrup
1 cup sugar
1 teaspoon vanilla
1⅓ cups creamy peanut butter
5 cups corn flakes

Cook syrup and sugar over low heat, stirring very frequently, until it comes to a clear rolling boil. Remove from heat. Stir in vanilla and peanut butter until creamy. Fold in cornflakes 1 cup at a time. Drop by tablespoon onto waxed paper. Cool.

Vicki Thomas, Lena

Peanut Brittle

3 cups sugar
1 cup white Karo Syrup
⅔ cup water
2 cups raw peanuts
¼ stick margarine
1 teaspoon salt
2 teaspoons baking soda

Mix sugar, syrup and water; cook to hard-ball stage (use a candy thermometer). Add peanuts. Continue to cook to hard-crack stage. Remove from heat. Stir in margarine, salt and baking soda. Beat until golden brown. Pour onto a buttered enameled top or galvanized tin. Stretch as it cools and break into pieces.

© Kent Whitaker

Chocolate Covered Watermelon Candy

1 small ripe watermelon
8 ounces bittersweet chocolate
1 tablespoon butter-flavored Crisco
Salt (optional)

This is a sweet, delicious candy that is worth the extra effort of dehydrating the watermelon. A dehydrator appliance can be used if desired.

Line baking sheet with aluminum foil. Preheat oven to 150° (or its lowest setting). Slice watermelon into rectangles (about 2x4-inches by ½-inch thick). Place slices on baking sheet touching (they will shrink while dehydrating). Place in oven for 10 to 12 hours or until no longer sticky to the touch; turning baking sheet every 2 hours and flip watermelon pieces after 5 hours cook time. When watermelon has been completely dehydrated, remove from oven. Place on a drying rack to cool completely (overnight is fine). Cut watermelon into consistent sizes, if desired. Melt chocolate with Crisco. Dip watermelon and place on waxed paper to dry. Sprinkle with a very small amount of salt while still wet. When all pieces have been dipped, place candy in refrigerator to set for 20 minutes. Store Chocolate Covered Watermelon Candy in an airtight container in the refrigerator.

Water Valley Watermelon Carnival
First weekend in August • Water Valley

The Water Valley Watermelon Carnival is a two day event, held the weekend of the first Saturday of August. We begin with crafts during the day Friday and end the day with a street dance. Saturday is filled with live music, the Big Melon competition, watermelon eating contest, food vendors, craft vendors and much more. It is a must do event!

662.473.1122 • watervalleychamber.info

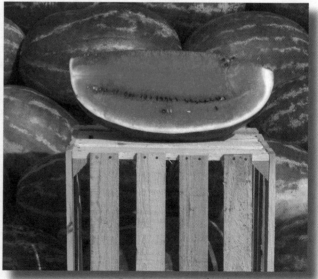

© Craig Leaper • image from bigstockphoto.com

Sweet Potato Candy

2 cups light brown sugar
¾ cup evaporated milk
1 tablespoon butter or margarine
½ cup chopped pecans
⅛ tablespoon salt
1 cup cooked sweet potatoes, mashed

Combine first 3 ingredients. Cook over medium heat to soft-ball stage; cool. Add remaining 3 ingredients; beat well. Pour into buttered pan; cool completely. Cut into squares.

Chocolate Covered Caramels

1 (14-ounce) package Kraft caramels
3 tablespoons water
2 cups chopped pecans or walnuts
8 large plain Hershey bars
⅓ bar paraffin
1 teaspoon vanilla

Melt caramels and water in double boiler. Add nuts and drop by spoonfuls on aluminum foil. Chill in refrigerator 30 minutes. Melt Hershey bars, paraffin and vanilla in a double boiler. Drop caramels in one at a time and coat with chocolate mixture. Place on waxed paper. Let set 5 minutes, and then enjoy.

Rose Compere, Mendenhall

Caramel Corn

6 quarts popped corn
1 cup margarine
2 cups brown sugar
½ cup Karo
   (light corn syrup)
1 teaspoon salt
½ teaspoon baking soda
1 teaspoon vanilla

Spread popped corn evenly in 2 large roasting pans; set aside. Melt margarine in large pot. Add brown sugar and syrup; stir well. Bring to boil; boil 5 minutes, stirring constantly. Continue to boil 5 minutes longer without stirring. Remove from heat. Stir in baking soda and vanilla. Slowly pour over popcorn. Mix well; bake at 250° for 1 hour, stirring every 15 minutes. Remove and cool. Break apart and store in airtight container.

Chocolate Candy

⅓ cup cocoa
3 cups sugar
Dash salt
1½ cups milk
¼ cup butter
1 teaspoon vanilla flavoring
1 cup chopped pecans, optional

Combine cocoa, sugar, salt and milk in heavy boiler. Cook until hard ball forms when a small amount is dropped in cold water. In a separate bowl, place butter and vanilla flavoring. Pour hot mixture in bowl. Cool about 5 minutes and add pecans. Beat with mixer until glossy then beat with hand while dropping on waxed paper. Cool before serving.

Francis Henderson, It

Bessie's Fudge

4½ cups sugar
Pinch salt
2 tablespoons butter
1 (12-ounce) can evaporated milk
2 (12-ounce) bags semisweet chocolate chips
2 (7-ounce) jars marshmallow creme
2 cups chopped nuts

Bessie Jackson was one of my grandmother's good friends. I found this recipe by Bessie in one of my grandmother's handwritten cookbooks. It seems that it was one of her favorite fudge recipes. – Kent

In a saucepan, combine first 4 ingredients and bring to a boil. Boil 4 to 5 minutes (do not scorch); remove from heat. Stir in chocolate, marshmallow creme and nuts; continue to stir until chocolate is melted. Spoon into pan lined with waxed paper. Chill several hours until thickened. Slice into pieces.

Bessie Jackson, Grenada

Martha Washington Candy

2 (16-ounce) boxes powdered sugar
1⅓ cups flaked coconut
1 can sweetened condensed milk
1 stick butter, softened
1 teaspoon vanilla
1 quart pecans
½ bar (2 ounces) paraffin
1 (16-ounce) package semi-sweet chocolate chips

Mix sugar, coconut, milk, butter, vanilla and pecans. Mixture will be very thick. Roll into little balls; chill (overnight, if possible). Melt paraffin and chocolate chips in double boiler. Dip balls into mixture one at a time. Lay on waxed paper to dry. May be frozen; thaw before serving.

Rose Compere, Mendenhall

Demaris Lee's Pecan Praline Crunch

1 (16-ounce) package Quaker Oat Cereal (8 cups)
2 cups pecan pieces
½ cup light corn syrup
½ cup firmly packed brown sugar
¼ cup margarine or butter (½ stick)
1 teaspoon vanilla
½ teaspoon baking soda

Heat oven to 250º. Combine cereal and pecans in a lightly sprayed 9x13-inch pan; set aside. Combine corn syrup, brown sugar and margarine in 2 cup microwavable bowl. Microwave on high for 1½ minutes; stir. Microwave on high ½ to 1½ minutes more or until boiling. Stir in vanilla and baking soda; pour over cereal mixture. Stir to coat evenly. Bake 1 hour, stirring every 10 minutes. Spread on baking sheet to cool; break into pieces.

Demaris Lee, Petal

Granny's Divinity

3 egg whites
3 cups sugar
½ cup water
½ cup white Karo˚
Pinch salt
1 teaspoon clear vanilla extract
1 cup chopped pecans
   (larger pieces, not finely chopped)

Beat egg whites until stiff; set aside. Combine sugar, water and Karo in a saucepan. Boil until mixture reaches hard ball stage. Pour ½ syrup over beaten egg whites, beating well. Continue beating egg white mixture while returning remaining syrup to heat; boil 1 minute. Continuing to beat, add remaining syrup to egg white mixture. Add vanilla extract and nuts. Continue to beat until candy looses it's gloss. Spoon onto waxed paper; serve when set.

Francis Henderson, It

Cakes & Cobblers

Butter Pecan Cake

1 butter pecan cake mix
4 eggs
1 cup oil
1 cup water
1 can coconut pecan frosting
1 cup pecans, chopped
1 cup coconut
½ package Golden Brand® raisins,
   softened in water

Mix cake mix, eggs, oil and water together. Stir in frosting. Then add pecans, coconut and raisins. Bake in bundt pan at 350° 1 hour or until done.

Leanne Townsend, Lena

Mom's Buttermilk Cake

1 cup Crisco (do not substitute)
2½ cups sugar
1 teaspoon vanilla
1 teaspoon almond extract
   (or lemon extract)
5 whole eggs
3 cups flour, sifted
1 cup buttermilk
¼ teaspoon baking soda
¼ cup boiling water

This is my mom's recipe for Buttermilk Cake from our Finfrock Family Fun Cookbook by my sister Carol. Mom stressed in the recipe, "Do not substitute the Crisco!"

Cream Crisco and sugar in large bowl. Add vanilla and almond extract; mix. Add eggs, at a time, stirring well after each. Alternate adding flour and buttermilk, beginning and ending with flour. Dissolve baking soda in boiling water; add to batter. Pour into a well-greased tube pan. Bake for about 1 hour at 350°.

L. Randall 'Randy' Finfrock and his mother
Lois Virginia Finfrock, Enterprise

Old-Fashioned Sour Cream Pound Cake

1½ cups butter, no substitute
3 cups sugar
6 large eggs, beaten
1 cup sour cream
3 cups flour, sifted
¼ teaspoon baking soda

Preheat oven to 325°. Cream butter and sugar. Add beaten eggs and sour cream. Combine flour and baking soda; gradually add to butter mixture. Beat until light and fluffy, about 2 minutes. Bake in greased and floured 10-inch tube pan for 1 hour and 10 minutes.

Delma Frazier Rodabough, Amory/McCool

© V.F. • image from bigstockphoto.com

Blueberry Pound Cake

1 cup butter, softened
2 cups sugar
4 eggs
1 teaspoon vanilla
3 cups all-purpose flour, divided
½ teaspoon salt
1 teaspoon baking powder
2 cups blueberries, fresh or frozen

Cream butter and sugar. Add eggs one at a time and beat until light and fluffy. Add vanilla. Sift 2 cups flour, salt and baking powder together. Add sifted ingredients to creamed mixture and beat. Dredge berries in remaining flour. Fold into batter. Pour into a tube pan which has been buttered and coated with sugar. Bake at 325° for 1 hour and 15 minutes.

Gulf South Blueberry Growers
Nesbit Blueberry Plantation, Hernando

© Alton Applewhite • image from istockphoto.com

Mississippi

Hospitality State Pound Cake

1 pound butter (4 sticks) plus ½ stick for topping
3 teaspoons butter flavoring
3 cups sugar
6 eggs
4 cups flour
¾ cup milk
3 to 4 teaspoons vanilla

Beat butter and butter flavoring until creamy and fluffy. Gradually add sugar and beat until light and fluffy. Add eggs, one at a time, beating well after adding each egg. Add flour alternately with milk, beginning and ending with flour. Stir in vanilla. Pour into greased and floured 10-inch tube pan or 2 loaf pans. Bake at 325° for 90 minutes. After cake is cooked, melt ½ stick butter and pour in cake's cracks while hot.

Rita Franklin, Hattiesburg

Mawmaw's Pound Cake for Jill

1 box Duncan Hines butter cake mix
5 eggs
1 (8-ounce) carton sour cream
½ cup canola oil
½ cup sugar
1 tablespoon melted margarine

Empty dry cake mix into a large bowl. Add remaining ingredients, one at a time, mixing well after each ingredient is added. Bake at 350° for 55 to 60 minutes in tube pan.

Jill Gregory, Madison

Milky Way Pound Cake

6 (2.15-ounce.) Milky Way candy bars
1 cup margarine, divided
2 cups sugar
4 eggs
2½ cups sifted all-purpose flour
½ teaspoon baking soda
1¼ cups buttermilk
1 cup chopped pecans

Preheat oven to 325°. Melt candy bars with ½ cup margarine in microwave or in top of double boiler. Set aside. In a large bowl, cream sugar and ½ cup margarine. Add eggs one at a time to creamed mixture, beating well after each addition. Sift flour and baking soda together. Add alternately with buttermilk to creamed mixture beating well. Stir in melted candy bars and pecans. Pour into greased and floured 10-inch tube pan. Bake 1 hour and 10 minutes. Cool 10 minutes and remove from pan. When completely cool, frost with Milky Way Icing.

Milky Way Icing:

3 (2.15-ounce) Milky Way candy bars
½ cup margarine
2 cups powdered sugar
1 to 2 tablespoons milk

Melt candy bars and margarine in microwave or in top of double boiler over low heat. Remove from heat and beat in sugar. Thin with milk until spreading consistency.

Delma Frazier Rodabough, Amory/McCool

Chocolate Chip Cake

1 (6-ounce) package chocolate chips
¾ cup chopped pecans
1 box yellow butter cake mix
    (without pudding)
4 eggs
½ cup oil
¼ cup water
1 teaspoon vanilla
1 small box instant vanilla pudding
1 (8-ounce) carton sour cream

Coat chocolate chips and pecans with a little of the dry cake mix. Combine remaining cake mix with eggs, oil, water, vanilla, vanilla pudding and sour cream thoroughly. Fold in chocolate chips and pecans. Pour into a greased and floured tube pan. Bake about 50 minutes at 350°. Cool before frosting.

Chocolate Frosting:

1 (16-ounce) box powdered sugar
3 squares baking chocolate, melted
¾ stick margarine, softened
Milk

Combine powdered sugar, melted chocolate and butter. Add enough milk to make the frosting of a spreading consistency. Frost cake and serve.

Alice M. Henderson, Florence

Lorraine's "Real" Mississippi Mud Cake

2 sticks butter or margarine
½ cup cocoa
2 cups sugar
4 eggs, slightly beaten
1½ cups all-purpose flour
¼ teaspoon salt
1½ cups chopped nuts
2 teaspoons vanilla
1 (10-ounce) bag miniature marshmallows

Melt butter with cocoa in a saucepan over medium heat. Remove from heat, cool slightly, and pour in a bowl. Stir in sugar and beaten eggs; mix well. Add flour, salt, nuts and vanilla while mixing well. Spoon batter into a greased 9x13-inch pan and bake at 350° for 35 to 45 minutes. Remove from oven. While hot, cover with marshmallows and frost.

Frosting:

1 pound powdered sugar
½ cup milk or cream
⅓ cup cocoa
½ stick butter or margarine, softened

Combine all ingredients; mix until smooth. Spread over Mississippi mud cake

Lorraine McCormick, Biloxi

Chopped Apple Cake

3 cups all-purpose flour
2 cups sugar
1 teaspoon baking soda
1 teaspoon salt
3 teaspoons cinnamon
3 eggs, well beaten
1 cup oil
1 cup chopped nuts
3 cups chopped apples

Sift together all 5 dry ingredients. Mix eggs, oil, nuts and apples; add to dry ingredients. Mix well and place in greased and floured tube pan. Bake at 350° for 1 hour.

Valerie, Biloxi

Grillin' for life
October • Madison

Visitors to this family festival can enjoy great BBQ cooked on site, along with musical entertainment, craft shopping and more. This BBQ Competition includes a chance for professionals and "backyard" teams to have their BBQ judged alongside their peers. It's a local event and an official Kansas City Barbeque Society competition.

601.214.9463 • grillinforlife.com

Mama's Fruit Cake

3 cups sugar
1 pound butter
12 eggs
2 teaspoons vanilla
2 teaspoons almond extract
1 teaspoon salt
2 teaspoons lemon juice
5 cups flour
2½ cups candied cherries
2½ cups candied pineapple
1 fresh coconut, grated
5 cups pecans

Cream sugar and butter. Add eggs, vanilla, almond extract, salt, lemon juice and flour. Mix in fruit, coconut and pecans. Bake in large pan at 250° about 1½ hours. This makes about 12 pounds of Fruit Cake.

Ethel Mae Musgrove, Florence

Apricot Nectar Cake

1 lemon supreme cake mix
1 (3.4-ounce) box instant lemon pudding
1 cup apricot nectar
⅓ cup vegetable oil
4 large eggs
1 cup powdered sugar
Lemon juice

I make this cake for all occasions. I frequently garnish it with lemon zest. At Christmas, I decorate it with cherries.

Combine cake mix, pudding mix, apricot nectar and oil. Add eggs one at a time mixing well after each. Mixture will be thick. Pour into a greased and floured tube or bunt pan. Bake at 350° for 40 to 45 minutes; cool. Combine powdered sugar with enough lemon juice to make glaze. Pour over top of cake.

Sara Albritton, Canton

Easy Coconut Cake

1 white cake mix
  plus ingredients to prepare according to package directions
1 (15-ounce) can cream of coconut
1 (14-ounce) can sweetened condensed milk
1 (8-ounce) carton Cool Whip
1 (7-ounce) bag coconut

Prepare and bake cake mix as directed, using only the egg whites, in a 9x13-inch pan. Cool. Poke holes in the top of the cake. Pour cream of coconut then sweetened condensed milk over top. Frost with Cool Whip. Sprinkle with coconut. Refrigerate until ready to serve.

Kristy Lepard, Good Hope

Demaris Lee's Pumpkin Cake

1 cup sugar
3 eggs, beaten
3 teaspoons cinnamon
1 (16-ounce) can pumpkin
1 (12-ounce) can evaporated milk
1 yellow cake mix
1 cup chopped pecans
1½ sticks margarine, melted

Preheat oven to 350°. Combine first 5 ingredients. Pour into 9x13-inch pan. Sprinkle dry cake mix then pecans on top. Pour melted margarine over top. Bake for 40 to 60 minutes. Cool before frosting.

Icing:
½ cup powdered sugar
1 (8-ounce) package cream cheese, softened
¾ cup Cool Whip

Cream sugar and cream cheese. Fold in Cool Whip. Spread on cool cake.

Demaris Lee, Petal

Peanut Butter Cake with PBC Frosting

1 cup smooth peanut butter
¾ cup butter or margarine
1½ cups sugar
4 eggs
1 tablespoon vanilla
2 cups flour
3 teaspoons baking powder
1 teaspoon salt
¼ teaspoon cinnamon
1 cup milk

With a electric mixer, cream peanut butter, butter and sugar. Add eggs then vanilla and mix by hand. Combine dry ingredients in separate bowl. Add dry ingredients to creamed mixture alternately with milk, stirring well with a spoon. Pour in a greased 9x13-inch pan. Bake at 350° for 35 to 40 minutes.

Peanut Butter Cocoa Frosting:

2 cups powdered sugar
⅓ cup cocoa
1½ cups peanut butter
1 teaspoon vanilla
6 to 7 tablespoons milk

Combine sugar and cocoa; add peanut butter and mix well. Add vanilla; mix. Continue to beat while adding milk, 1 tablespoon at a time, to spreading consistency. Spread over cooled cake. YUM-YUM!

John Stamoulis USCG in honor of his grandmother,
Tina Kennedy, Gulfport

Hot Fudge Lava Cake

1 cup flour
1¾ cups sugar, divided
4 tablespoons cocoa, divided
½ cup milk
3 tablespoons butter, melted
1 teaspoon vanilla
1½ cups boiling water

Combine flour, ¾ cup sugar and 2 tablespoons cocoa. Add milk, butter and vanilla; mix well. Pour into 8-inch square baking dish. In a separate bowl, combine 1 cup sugar and 2 tablespoons cocoa; sprinkle over cake batter. Pour boiling water over the top; DO NOT STIR. Bake at 350º for 35 minutes.

Leanne Townsend, Lena

Chocolate Chip Cookie Dough Cake

2 rolls chocolate chip cookie dough
2 (8-ounce) packages cream cheese, softened
3 eggs
1 cup sugar

Press one roll chocolate chip cookie dough in bottom of a 9x13-inch pan. Combine cream cheese, eggs and sugar together; spread over cookie dough in pan. Crumble remaining roll cookie dough over top. Bake at 375º for 40 minutes. Cool before cutting.

Brittany Harrison, Lena

Orange-Pineapple Cake

Cake:

1 box butter cake mix
**   plus ingredients to prepare per package directions**
1 can mandarin oranges

Mix cake as directed on box; add oranges with juice. Pour into treated 9x13-inch pan. Bake at 350° until done. Cool before frosting.

Frosting:

1 (3.4-ounce) package instant vanilla pudding
1 can crushed pineapple
1 (8-ounce) carton Cool Whip

Combine dry pudding mix and pineapple. Fold in Cool Whip. Refrigerate until ready to serve.

Leanne Townsend, Lena

Antebellum Home
Natchez

© Mosaikphotography • image from istockphoto.com

Heavenly Baby Ruth Cake

1 chocolate cake mix
    plus ingredients to prepare per package directions
1 cup creamy peanut butter
6 (2.1-ounce) Baby Ruth candy bars, chopped
½ cup butter or margarine
1 cup evaporated milk
1 cup sugar
2 large egg yolks

Preheat oven to 350°. Lightly grease and flour 9x13-inch baking pan. Prepare cake mix batter according to package directions; stir in peanut butter. Pour into prepared pan. Bake 30 to 40 minutes or until wooden pick inserted in center comes out clean. Cool completely in pan on wire rack. Place chopped candy bars and butter in medium-sized heavy-duty saucepan. Cook over low heat, stirring frequently, until candy bars are melted. Combine evaporated milk, sugar and egg yolks in medium bowl. Add to Baby Ruth mixture. Cook over medium heat, stirring frequently, about 10 more minutes or until thickened. Cool in refrigerator 30 minutes; stir. Frost cake. Refrigerate until ready to serve. Makes 15 servings.

V. Rayburn, Florence

Red Velvet Cake

½ cup Crisco
1½ cups sugar
2 eggs
1 teaspoon vanilla
1 teaspoon butter flavoring
3 tablespoons cocoa
1 (½-ounce) bottle red coloring
1 teaspoon salt
2½ cups sifted flour
1 cup buttermilk
1 teaspoon baking soda
1 tablespoon vinegar

Cream shortening, sugar, eggs and flavorings. Make a paste of cocoa and food coloring; add to first mixture. Add salt. Alternately add flour and buttermilk; mixing well. Combine baking soda and vinegar in small bowl; add to batter. Blend. Add evenly to 3 (9- or 10-inch) greased and floured cake pans. Bake at 350º for 20 to 25 minutes or until done. Cool completely.

Frosting:

2 cups milk
6 tablespoons flour
1 teaspoon salt
2 cups Crisco (not butter flavored)
2 cups sugar
4 teaspoons vanilla
1 teaspoon butter flavoring

Cook milk, flour and salt until thick, stirring constantly; cool to room temperature. Cream shortening and sugar very well. Add flavorings. Add cooked mixture and beat well. Spread on cooled cake.

Note: When making the cake, I always cook the milk and flour mixture for the frosting first and set it aside to cool. By the time the cake bakes and cools this cooked mixture is cool also. About twenty years ago this cake won me first prize (blue ribbon) at the county fair.

Rita S. Franklin, Hattiesburg

Robbie's Red Velvet Cake

2½ cups self-rising flour
1½ cups sugar
1 teaspoon baking soda
1 teaspoon cocoa
1 cup buttermilk
1 teaspoon vanilla
1½ cups cooking oil
2 eggs
1 (3-ounce) bottle red food coloring

This recipe is from the late Robbie Pope, a well loved member of the Flower Lovers Garden Club of Amory. It is the best that I have ever tasted.

Sift together dry ingredients. Add remaining ingredients, in order, mixing thoroughly after each. Pour in 3 cake pans that have been greased and floured. Bake at 350° for 25 minutes or until cake springs back when pressed in the middle.

Frosting:

1 stick real butter, softened
1 (8-ounce) package cream cheese, softened
1 box powdered sugar
½ teaspoon vanilla
Chopped nuts, optional

Mix and spread on cooled cake. Sprinkle chopped nuts on top and sides, if desired. Keep in refrigerator.

Sandra Neal in honor of Robbie Pope, Amory

Lemon Jelly Cake

1 cup butter
2 cups sugar
3 cups flour
3 teaspoons baking powder
½ teaspoon salt
¾ cup milk
1 teaspoon vanilla
6 egg whites, stiffly beaten

Cream butter and sugar, beating until light and fluffy. Add sifted dry ingredients alternately with milk. Add vanilla. Fold in stiffly beaten egg whites. Pour into 3 greased round 9-inch layer pans. Bake at 350° for 25 or 30 minutes, or until top springs back when touched. Cool on racks

Lemon Jelly Filling:

½ cup butter
1 cup sugar
6 egg yolks
Grated rind of 2 lemons
Juice of 2 lemons

Combine all ingredients in top of double boiler. Cook over hot water, stirring constantly until thick, about 20 to 25 minutes. Cool completely, then put in freezer 7 minutes. Spread between layers of cake and ice top and sides with Seven Minute Frosting (see next page).

Seven Minute Frosting

3 egg whites
5 tablespoons water
¼ cup white Karo syrup
Dash salt
Dash cream of tartar
1½ cups sugar
1 teaspoon vanilla flavoring

When I was growing up, this yummy icing was always on a layered chocolate cake. It's a delicious taste of my childhood. – Sheila

Put all ingredients, except vanilla flavoring, into a double-boiler over boiling water (or use a saucepan in a skillet with boiling water). Beat continuously with an electric mixes until stiff peaks form, about 7 minutes. Remove from heat and beat in vanilla flavoring. Continue beating until frosting is thick and smooth. (Just starts to lose its gloss). Spread on cake immediately while frosting is still soft and smooth.

Anita Musgrove, Brandon

Chocolate Frosting

⅓ cup cocoa
3 cups sugar
Dash salt
1½ cups milk
¼ cup butter
1 teaspoon vanilla flavoring
1 cup chopped pecans, optional

Combine cocoa, sugar, salt and milk in heavy boiler. Cook until soft ball forms in cold water. Put butter and vanilla flavoring in a bowl. Pour hot mixture in bowl. Let cool about 5 minutes and add pecans. Beat with mixer until glossy then ice cake.

Francis Henderson, It

Hummingbird Cake

3 cups all-purpose flour
2 cups sugar
1 teaspoon baking soda
1 teaspoon salt
1½ cups canola oil
3 eggs
1 (8-ounce) can crushed pineapple, drained
2 cups mashed bananas
1 cup chopped black walnuts
1 (8-ounce) package cream cheese, softened
1 stick butter, softened
1 pound powdered sugar
1 teaspoon vanilla extract

Preheat oven to 350°. Grease and flour 2 9-inch cake pans. Sift together flour, sugar, baking soda and salt. Set aside. In a large bowl, combine oil, eggs, pineapple, bananas and nuts. Add flour mixture, and mix together by hand. Pour batter into prepared pans and bake 1 hour or until a toothpick inserted in center comes out clean. Remove from oven and allow to cool on racks. Prepare frosting by blending together cream cheese, butter, powdered sugar and vanilla until smooth. Evenly spread frosting on middle, sides and top of cake.

Strawberry Plains Festival

Strawberry Cake & Icing

1 box white cake mix
1 tablespoon all-purpose flour
1 (3-ounce) package strawberry Jell-O
¾ cup oil
½ cup water
½ cup frozen strawberries,
   thawed (to mushy stage)
4 eggs

Icing:
½ pound (2 sticks) butter, softened
1 pound powdered sugar
½ cup frozen strawberries

Combine dry cake mix and flour. Add Jell-O, oil, water and strawberries; mix thoroughly. Add one egg at a time, beating with an electric mixer after each, until all 4 eggs have been added. Divide batter between 2 9-inch cake pans. Bake at 350° for 35 minutes. Cool before icing. Gradually add powdered sugar to softened butter. Add strawberries. Blend and spread over cake.

Teresa Vanlandingham, Brandon

Strawberry Plains Festival
Weekend following Labor Day • Holly Springs

Visit one of Mississippi's finest natural treasures every fall for this premier nature festival. Witness migrating Ruby-Throated Hummingbirds as they stop to refuel on their journey from Canada to their winter home in Mexico and Central America. Look close as these tiny birds are caught and banded right before your eyes. You may even be lucky enough to release one back into the wild! Also enjoy live animal demonstrations, kids' tent, guided wagon rides, and renowned guest speakers! It's the Hummingbird Migration Celebration and Nature Festival at Strawberry Plains Audubon Center in Holly Springs, MS, always held on the weekend after Labor Day.

662.252.1155 • strawberryplains.audubon.org

Strawberry Cake

1 box strawberry cake mix
   plus ingredients to prepare per directions on box
1 can sweetened condensed milk
1 large package frozen strawberries in juice,
   thawed (divided)
1 (8-ounce) package cream cheese, softened
2 cups powdered sugar
1 (8-ounce) tub Cool Whip

Bake cake as directed on box in a 9x13-inch pan. As soon as you take it out of the oven, poke holes in the cake with a tooth pick. Pour sweetened condensed milk and ½ strawberries over top. Cool. Combine cream cheese and sugar. Fold in Cool Whip and remaining strawberries. Top cake with frosting and store in fridge.

Leanne Townsend, Lena

Roosevelt State Park
Morton

© Doyle Hastings

Stephanie's Easy Coconut Cake

1 box Duncan Hines Golden Butter Cake Mix
   plus ingredients to prepare per package directions
8 ounces sour cream
2 cups sugar
3 (6-ounce) packages frozen coconut, thawed
1 (8-ounce) carton Cool Whip

Prepare and bake cake according to directions in 2 layers; cool completely. Split layers to make 4 layers. While cake is cooling, combine sour cream, sugar and 2 packages coconut. Spread between cake layers.. Cover top and sides with Cool Whip and sprinkle remaining coconut on top and sides.

Stephanie Jackson, Faulkner

Old Fashioned Peach Cobbler

2 large cans peaches
   (or 6 fresh peaches cooked down)
2 cups sugar, divided
2 sticks margarine, divided
1½ cups self-rising flour
1 cup milk

Cook peaches down with ½ cup sugar until tender. Stir in 1 stick margarine, set aside to cool slightly. Mix flour and remaining 1½ cups sugar. Grease a 9x13-inch casserole dish with margarine. Cut remaining margarine into flour and sugar. Pour peaches into dish; top with flour mixture. Cook at 375° until golden brown, about 30 minutes. Serve with ice cream of your choice.

Luann Richardson, Brandon

Muscadine Cobbler

1 pint muscadines
1 stick margarine
½ cup flour
¾ cup sugar
½ cup milk

Cook muscadines in a little water over medium heat, until cooked down. Preheat oven to 350°. Put 1 stick margarine in dish in oven until melted. Combine flour, sugar and milk; pour over butter in dish. Pour muscadines over batter; do not stir. Bake 35 to 40 minutes or until set.

Delma Frazier Rodabough,
Amory/McCool

Mamaw's EZ Peach Cobbler

1 cup self-rising flour
1 cup milk
1 cup sugar
   (can substitute Splenda)
1 can sliced peaches
¼ stick butter
2 teaspoons cinnamon, optional
Vanilla ice cream, optional

This was my grandmother's recipe. She taught me to make it when I was 19 and just married. It's very easy and I couldn't ruin it no matter what. Now that I'm 56 years old and have Type 2 Diabetes, I still make Mamaw's EZ Peach Cobbler using Splenda instead of sugar. It's just as good. Mamaw knows best!

Combine flour, milk and sugar; stir in peaches. Pour into baking dish. Top with tabs of butter, and sprinkle with cinnamon. Cook at 350° about 20 minutes or until top turns slightly brown. Remove from oven and let sit for 5 minutes or so. Delicious! Serve with vanilla ice cream for a real sweet treat.

Brenda Fiscus, Lena

Peach Cobbler

½ cup unsalted butter
1 cup all-purpose flour
2 cups sugar, divided
1 tablespoon baking powder
Pinch salt
1 cup milk
1 tablespoon lemon juice
4 cups fresh peaches, sliced (or canned and drained)
½ teaspoon ground cinnamon

Melt butter in 9x13-inch pan. Combine flour, 1 cup sugar, baking powder and salt. Add milk; stir just until blended. Pour in pan with butter. DON'T STIR. Bring remaining 1 cup sugar and lemon juice to a boil; add peaches and cinnamon. Pour over batter. Bake at 375º for 40 to 45 minutes or until brown. Yield 10 servings.

Chef Matt Huffman, Executive Chef
for the Governor of Mississippi, Jackson

Muscadine Jubilee
Second Saturday in September • Pelahatchie

For 25 years, thousands of people have been coming to Pelahatchie late in the summer to pay homage to the muscadine grape, famed ingredient in southern wines, pies, and jellies. The Muscadine Jubilee is Pelahatchie's premier event. The event begins with the Mayor's Prayer Breakfast. Later, the crowds assemble at Muscadine Park for food, fun, arts and crafts, music, and of course, the Grape Stomp!

601.854.5224 • pelahatchie.org

Oreo Cheesecake

1 package Oreo chocolate
   sandwich cookies
¼ cup butter, melted
4 (8-ounce) packages cream cheese,
   softened
1 cup sugar
1 teaspoon vanilla
1 cup sour cream
4 eggs

Preheat oven 325°. Line 9x13-inch pan with foil. Process 30 cookies in food processor for 30 to 45 seconds or until finely ground. Add butter; mix well. Press firmly onto bottom of pan. Beat cream cheese, sugar and vanilla in a large bowl with electric mixer on medium speed. Add sour cream; mix well. Add eggs, 1 at a time, beating just until blended after each addition. Chop remaining cookies. Gently stir 1½ cups cookie crumbs into cream cheese batter. Pour over crust; sprinkle with remaining chopped cookies. Bake 40 minutes or until center is set. Cool. Refrigerate 4 hours before serving.

Leanne Townsend, Lena

Amaretto Cheesecake

1 (8-ounce) package cream cheese,
   softened
⅓ cup sugar
1 cup sour cream
2 teaspoons vanilla
¼ cup amaretto
1 (8-ounce) carton Cool Whip
1 graham cracker pie crust

Beat cheese until smooth; gradually beat in sugar. Blend in sour cream, vanilla and amaretto. Fold in whipped topping, blending well. Spoon into crust. Chill until set, at least 4 hours.

Virginia Hammon

Pies & Other Desserts

Aunt Ouida's Chocolate Pie page 213

Our Favorite Chocolate Pie

3 tablespoons cocoa powder
2 cups sugar
2 teaspoons flour
1 teaspoon salt
3 eggs, beaten
¾ cup evaporated milk
½ cup butter, melted
1 teaspoon Watkins double-strength vanilla extract
1 frozen deep-dish pie crust

In large mixing bowl, mix cocoa, sugar, flour and salt. Whisk in eggs, milk, butter and vanilla. Mix by hand or mixer on low about 2 minutes. Pour into frozen deep-dish pie crust. Bake in 350º oven 40 to 45 minutes, or until a toothpick inserted in the middle comes out clean. (The center will no longer wiggle.) Place tin foil pieces over pie crust edges to prevent the crust from burning. Cool completely.

Meringue:

3 egg whites
¼ teaspoon cream of tartar
6 tablespoons sugar
½ teaspoon Watkins® double-strength vanilla
1 dash salt

Beat egg whites and cream of tartar in medium bowl with electric mixer on high speed until foamy. Add sugar, 1 tablespoon at a time; add vanilla and a dash of salt. Beat about 8 minutes until it makes a whipped cream. Frost top of pie completely. Place in oven set to broil; leave the oven cracked, so you can watch carefully. Leave pie in oven about 1 minute, until meringue is barely starting to turn brown. This is giving it that toasted marshmallow look. Remove immediately. Cool uncovered for about an hour. You can refrigerate pie or leave in a cake or pie plate with the cover on.

Stephanie Jackson, Faulkner

Chocolate Chess Pie

1 stick butter
3½ tablespoons Hershey's cocoa
1½ cups sugar
2 eggs, beaten
1 small can Pet milk
   (evaporated milk)
1 teaspoon vanilla
1 pie crust, unbaked

This has been passed down from a lot of generations and is a family favorite. We normally have to make two so everyone can have seconds.

Melt butter and add cocoa; remove from heat. Add sugar. Combine eggs, milk and vanilla separately, then add to cocoa mixture. Mix thoroughly. Pour into pie crust and bake at 325° approximately 55 minutes.

Teresa Vanlandingham, Brandon

Aunt Ouida's Chocolate Pie

1 pie shell
1 cup sugar
3 tablespoons cocoa
5½ tablespoons flour
2 cups milk, divided
3 eggs, beaten
⅓ stick butter
½ teaspoon vanilla
2 egg whites
Salt
Cream of tartar

Place pie shell in pie pan; pinch edges and prick bottom and sides with fork. Place foil collar over edges to keep from burning. Bake 10 minutes at 350°; do not brown. Cool. In saucepan, mix sugar, cocoa and flour. Add ½ cup milk to make a paste. Slowly add 3 beaten whole eggs and remaining milk, stirring well. Add butter. Heat in double boiler, stirring constantly, until thickened. Remove from heat. Add vanilla; set aside to cool. To prepare meringue, add pinch of salt and cream of tartar to egg whites. Beat at high speed until stiff. Fill pie shell with chocolate mixture. Top with meringue, sealing to edges. Bake at 350° for 15 to 20 minutes.

L. Randall 'Randy' Finfrock and his Aunt Ouida, Enterprise

Mississippi Mud Pie

1 cup powdered sugar
1 cup semi-sweet chocolate morsels
¼ cup (½ stick) butter or margarine, cut up
¼ cup heavy whipping cream
2 tablespoons light corn syrup
1 teaspoon vanilla extract
¾ cup chopped pecans or walnuts, divided (optional)
2 pints coffee ice cream, softened slightly (divided)
1 (8-ounce) carton Cool Whip
1 (8-inch) chocolate crumb crust

Heat sugar, chocolate morsels, butter, cream and corn syrup in small, heavy-duty saucepan over low heat, stirring constantly, until butter is melted and mixture is smooth. Remove from heat. Stir vanilla extract into the chocolate sauce mixture. Cool until slightly warm. Drizzle ⅓ cup in bottom of crust; sprinkle with ¼ cup nuts. Layer 1 pint ice cream, scooping thin slices with a large spoon; freeze 1 hour. Repeat with ⅓ cup sauce, ¼ cup nuts and ice cream. Drizzle with remaining sauce; top with remaining nuts. Freeze 2 hours or until firm. Top with Cool Whip before serving.

Mandarin Orange Pie

1 can sliced Mandarin oranges,
**   drained**
1 (8-ounce) tub Cool Whip
1 (16-ounce) tub sour cream
1 can condensed milk
½ cup Tang
**   (powdered orange drink mix)**
2 graham cracker pie crusts

Combine all ingredients, except pie crusts. Divide mixture evenly between crusts. Refrigerate at least 2 hours or overnight.

Mary Carter, Yazoo City

Mama Frock's Lemon Meringue Pie

3 eggs, separated
Salt
¼ teaspoon cream of tartar
1 (7-ounce) jar marshmallow cream
1 large lemon
1⅓ cups sugar
6 tablespoons cornstarch
2 tablespoons butter
1 pie shell, cooked

Soon after my mom, Lois, became a grandmother, she was known thereafter as "Mama Frock" because the little ones in the family could not yet say our last name... Finfrock. This is her pie recipe from my sister Carol's Finfrock Family Fun Cookbook. Hope you enjoy!

Prepare meringue: Beat egg whites with salt and cream of tartar until foamy. Add marshmallow cream; beat until stiff peaks form. Set aside. Prepare Filling: Grate lemon; set rind aside. Squeeze juice of lemon into measuring cup. Add water to make ⅓ cup liquid; set aside. Beat egg yolks; set aside. Boil 1½ cups water in a small saucepan. In a large saucepan, combine sugar, cornstarch and pinch of salt. Stir in boiling water gradually, stirring until mixture thickens and is clear (about 1 minute). Stir 3 tablespoons sugar mixture into egg yolks. Add egg yolks back into sugar mixture. Cook over medium heat 3 minutes, stirring constantly. Stir in lemon juice, butter, and reserved rind. Pour into pie shell. Top with meringue, being careful to seal meringue to the sides of the crust. Bake at 350° for 12 to 15 minutes, or until meringue is golden.

L. Randall 'Randy' Finfrock and his mother Lois Virginia Finfrock, Enterprise

© Mathieu Boivin • image by istockphoto.com

Fresh Strawberry Pie

 1 quart whole strawberries
1 cup sugar
5 tablespoons cornstarch
7 ounces lemon-lime soda
Red food coloring, if desired
Prepared pie crust, baked and cooled

Trim tops from strawberries, rinse well, and set aside to dry. Blend sugar and cornstarch in a saucepan; add lemon-lime soda. Cook, stirring constantly, until smooth and thick. Add strawberries and cook another 5 minutes being sure that strawberries do not break down. If desired, add red food coloring. Pour into cooled pie shell. Chill.

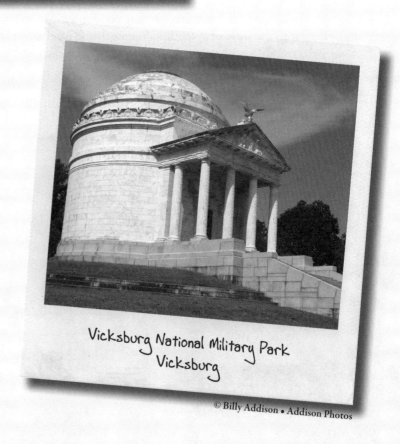

Vicksburg National Military Park
Vicksburg

© Billy Addison • Addison Photos

Mississippi

Homemade Sweet Potato Pie

2 cups mashed cooked sweet potatoes
6 tablespoons unsalted butter, softened
2 eggs, beaten
⅔ cup sugar
1 teaspoon vanilla extract
¼ teaspoon cinnamon
¼ cup evaporated milk
1 (9-inch) deep-dish pie shell, partially baked

Preheat oven to 350°. In a bowl, combine sweet potatoes and butter. Add eggs, sugar, vanilla, cinnamon and evaporated milk; stir well until smooth. Pour into pie shell and smooth top. Bake on a cookie sheet 25 to 35 minutes.

Alice M. Henderson, Florence

Coconut Pies

2 (9-inch) pie crusts
5 large eggs
2 cups sugar
¾ cup buttermilk
1 (7-ounce) package flake coconut

Bake crust per package directions; cool. Cream eggs and sugar. Add buttermilk. Stir in coconut. Pour evenly into 2 pie shells. Bake at 350° for 30 minutes or until set. Freezes very well.

Ida Williams

Guber's Old-Fashioned Coconut Pie

2 sticks margarine, softened
1½ cups sugar
3 eggs
1 tablespoon vinegar
    (1 tablespoon, not ANY more)
1 teaspoon vanilla
1 cup (or little over) coconut
(9-inch) deep pie shell

Blend margarine, sugar and eggs. Add vinegar, vanilla and coconut; mix well. Add to unbaked pie shell. Bake at 325° for 1 hour.

Betty Davis, Fulton

MawMaw Davis' Best Pecan Pie Ever!

1 stick margarine or butter
1 cup Golden Eagle Syrup
    (Not any other kind!)
1 cup sugar
3 large eggs, beaten
½ teaspoon lemon juice
1 teaspoon vanilla
Dash salt
1 cup chopped pecans
1 (8- or 9-inch) pie shell

Brown butter in pan until golden brown, do not burn; cool. In a separate bowl, combine ingredients, except pie crust, in order listed above; stir. Blend in browned (cooled) butter. Pour in unbaked pie shell and bake at 425° for 10 minutes; then lower oven to 325° and continue to cook 45 minutes or until done.

Dana Gregory, Florence

Thelma's Pecan Pie

1 cup white Karo syrup
1 cup sugar
3 eggs, well beaten
1 tablespoon melted butter
1 cup pecans (more or less)
1 teaspoon vanilla
1 pie shell

Mix all ingredients, except pie shell. Pour into pie shell. Bake at 350° for 45 to 60 minutes.

Frances Page,
Daughter-in-law of Thelma Page, Grenada

© Marie C. Fields • image from istockphoto.com

Mississippi Pecan Festival
Last weekend in September • Richton

Enjoy some of the South's finest foods. Shop at over 225 booths from all over the region. Sit and enjoy the most exciting stage in Mississippi. Listen to Bluegrass and Gospel music in the shade of huge pecan trees. Enjoy all the events that have made the MS Pecan Festival the favorite among families. You'll find the Mississippi Pecan Festival nestled in a shady pecan orchard six miles out of Richton, MS. The rich canopy supplied by the pecan trees makes it a perfect setting for such an event.

601.964.8201 • mspecanfestival.com

Stephanie's Fried Apple Pies

2 apples
⅓ cup sugar
½ teaspoon ground cinnamon
2 cups all-purpose flour
1 teaspoon salt
½ cup shortening
½ cup cold water
1 cup vegetable oil
Powdered sugar

Peel and dice apples. Add sugar and cinnamon. Cook in a saucepan over low heat until soft. Mash with fork to form a thick applesauce. Sift flour and salt together. Cut in shortening. Add water and mix with fork. Roll out to about ⅛-inch thick on a floured board. Cut with a large round cookie cutter (4 inches in diameter). In each round, place 1 heaping tablespoon fruit. Moisten edges with cold water, fold and press edge with a fork. Heat oil in a large skillet over medium-high heat. Fry pies, a few at a time, 2 to 3 minutes on each side; cook until golden brown. Drain on paper towels. Sprinkle with powdered sugar.

Stephanie Jackson, Faulkner

© antares71 • image from istockphoto.com

Grandmother's Pumpkin Dessert

3 eggs, beaten
1 (29-ounce) can pumpkin
1 (12-ounce) can evaporated milk
1 cup sugar
1 teaspoon nutmeg
2 teaspoons cinnamon
¼ teaspoon salt
1 box yellow cake mix
1¼ cups melted butter

The Mitchell family would like to share this recipe in memory of their grandmother Clara Mitchell.

Combine eggs, pumpkin, milk, sugar, nutmeg, cinnamon and salt. Spread evenly in a greased and floured baking dish. Sprinkle cake mix over top. Pour melted butter over top. Bake at 350° for 40 to 50 minutes.

Mitchell Family

Husband's Delight

1 cup flour
1 stick butter, softened
1 cup chopped nuts (or more for topping, if desired)
1 cup powdered sugar
1 (8-ounce) package cream cheese, softened
1 (16-ounce) carton Cool Whip, divided
1 package instant chocolate pudding
4 cups milk, divided
1 package instant vanilla pudding

Combine flour, butter and nuts. Press into bottom of 9x13-inch pan treated with non-stick spray. Bake at 350° until brown; cool. Combine powdered sugar and cream cheese with a mixer. Stir in 1 cup Cool Whip. Spread in cooled crust. Beat chocolate pudding and 2 cups milk until thick (about 2 minutes); spread over cream cheese layer. Combine vanilla pudding and 2 cups milk until thick; spread over chocolate layer. Top with remaining Cool Whip and sprinkle with additional pecans, if desired. Chill before serving.

Joy Sumerall, Raymond

Paula & Tascha's Blueberry Dessert

1 cup self-rising flour
1 stick margarine, melted
1 cup chopped pecans
1 (8-ounce) package cream cheese
1½ cups powdered sugar
1 (16-ounce) carton Cool Whip
1 cup sugar
3 tablespoons cornstarch
3 tablespoons grape Jell-O
1 cup water
¼ teaspoon almond extract
1 quart blueberries
1 cup toasted and chopped pecans

For the bottom layer, mix flour, margarine and 1 cup pecans; press into a 9x13-inch pan. Bake at 400° about 13 to 14 minutes or until golden brown; cool. Meanwhile, blend cream cheese and powdered sugar. Add ½ Cool Whip and blend until smooth. Spread over cooled crust. Refrigerate until firm. In saucepan, combine sugar, cornstarch and Jell-O; add water. Whisk together well. Cook over medium heat, stirring constantly, until mixture thickens, about 3 minutes. Stir in almond extract. Stir in fresh blueberries. If you prefer crisp berries, continue to cook only until heated through. Cook an extra 2 to 3 minutes if you prefer softer berries. Cool. Pour over cream cheese layer. Refrigerate until firm. Then top with remaining Cool Whip. Finish with a layer of toasted chopped pecans.

Gulf South Blueberry Growers
B&M Blueberry Farm, Purvis

Blueberry Nut Crunch

1 (30-ounce) can sliced peaches
3 to 4 cups fresh or frozen blueberries
1 cup sugar, divided
1 box yellow cake mix
1 stick margarine, melted
1 cup coarsely chopped almonds

Spray a 9x13-inch glass dish with cooking spray. Pour in peaches (with juice) and blueberries. Sprinkle with ¾ cup sugar then dry cake mix. Pour melted margarine over cake mix. Sprinkle with nuts and remaining ¼ sugar. Bake at 350° for 35 to 40 minutes. About midway through cooking time, cut slits in the top to allow juices to flow.

Gulf South Blueberry Growers
Arnold's Blueberry Farm, Hattiesburg

Red White and Blueberry Festival
First Weekend in June • Ocean Springs

Each year, Ocean Springs Fresh Market and Chamber hosts its Annual Red, White & Blueberry Festival in the L&N Depot parking lot in downtown Ocean Springs. The public is invited to enjoy free vanilla ice-cream topped with their choice of blueberries, strawberries or cherries provided by the Ocean Springs Chamber of Commerce Main Street Tourism Bureau, sample some great blueberry dishes, share blueberry recipes, purchase blueberry bushes and more. The Ocean Springs Fresh Market vendors will be out in full force with great local items for purchase. Cooking demonstrations and samples will be provided by local restaurants. Event is free to the public.

228.875.4424 • oceanspringschamber.com

Dolly's Blueberry Delight

1 angel food cake
1 (20-ounce) can unsweetened pineapple chunks
1½ cups blueberries, divided
1 (6-ounce) carton yogurt, your favorite fruit flavor
1 (16-ounce) carton Cool Whip
   (you will need only ⅔ of the carton)
½ teaspoon apple pie spice

In a large mixing bowl, break angel food cake in 2-inch chunks. Drain pineapple, reserving juice. Add drained pineapple, 1 cup blueberries and yogurt to cake; toss lightly. Add ½ pineapple juice; toss. Stir in ⅓ Cool Whip. Shake bowl to settle mixture. Top with about ½ remaining Cool Whip. Add remaining blueberries on top. Sprinkle with apple spice. Serve.

Gulf South Blueberry Growers
Firkaly Farms, Poplarville

Blueberry Crunch

Crust:
2 sticks butter, melted
2 cups flour
1 cup nuts

Filling:
1 (8-ounce) package cream cheese, softened
1 box powdered sugar
1 (16-ounce) carton Cool Whip
2 cans blueberry pie filling

Combine crust ingredients. Press down into 9x13-inch pan and bake at 350º for 30 minutes; cool. Beat cream cheese and powdered sugar with mixer. Fold in Cool Whip. Spread on crust and refrigerate a while. Then put blueberry filling on top and refrigerate again until your ready to eat.

Krista Griffin, Carthage

Punch Bowl Dessert

2 boxes banana pudding
    plus ingredients to prepare per directions on box
1 box yellow cake mix (pudding in mix)
    plus ingredients to prepare per directions on box
2 cans crushed pineapple, drained
1 (14- to 16-ounce) container frozen sliced strawberries
6 bananas, chopped
1 can sliced pineapple, drained or additional strawberries for topping

Prepare pudding per directions on box; chill in refrigerator. Prepare and bake cake per directions on box. Crumble ½ cake in bottom of punch bowl. Layer with ½ pudding, ½ crushed pineapple, ½ strawberries with juice and ½ bananas. Repeat layers. Top with sliced pineapple.

Kristy Lepard, Good Hope

© Keith Eddleman • image from istockphoto.com

Strawberry Pretzel Dessert

2 cups crushed pretzels
6 tablespoons sugar, divided
1¼ sticks butter, melted
1 (8-ounce) package cream cheese, softened
1 (8-ounce) container Cool Whip
2 (3-ounce) packages strawberry Jell-O
2 (10-ounce) cartons frozen, sweetened strawberries

Mix pretzels, 3 tablespoons sugar and melted butter. Press into 9x13-inch pan. Bake at 350° for 8 to 10 minutes; cool. In a separate bowl, beat cream cheese with remaining 3 tablespoons sugar. Gently fold in Cool Whip. Spread over cooled crust and chill. Dissolve Jell-O in 2 cups boiling water. Stir in strawberries. Pour over cream cheese. Chill.

Pam Simpson, Vancleave

Grilled Fruit with Sweet and Sour Sauce

8 assorted fruits (apple, peach, pears etc.)
¼ cup balsamic vinegar
½ cup sour cream
½ cup mayonnaise
¼ cup honey
2 tablespoons soy sauce
¼ cup sugar
1 teaspoon cinnamon

Cut fruits in half. Brush fruit with vinegar and place on grill flesh down. Allow to cook until flesh softens, about 20 to 30 minutes. Combine sour cream, mayonnaise, honey and soy sauce. Mix cinnamon and sugar together. After removing fruit from grill, top with a dollop of sauce and sprinkle with sugar mixture. This is great served with homemade ice cream.

Steven Stolk, Brandon

Creamy Banana Pudding

1 (14-ounce) can sweetened condensed milk
1½ cups cold water
1 (4-ounce) package instant vanilla pudding
2 cups (1 pint) whipping cream, whipped
3 teaspoons vanilla wafers
Sliced bananas to taste

In large bowl, combine sweetened condensed milk and water. Add pudding mix; beat well. Chill 5 minutes. Fold in whipped cream. Spoon ⅓ pudding mixture into 2½ quart glass serving bowl. Top with ½ each wafers and bananas. Repeat layers. Finish with remaining ⅓ pudding. Chill thoroughly. Refrigerate leftovers.

Donna Monroe, Greenville

Wild Game Cook-Off
Last weekend in February • Tunica

Wild Game Cook-Off is a Festival that is held in downtown Tunica. Teams set up and decorate their "kitchens" and start cooking. Everything must be cooked on site. Cash prizes and trophies are given as prizes. We start in the morning with drink categories and then go to small and large game, hot wings and chili. Competition is fierce.

662.363.6611 • tunicamainstreet.com

Quick and Easy Banana Pudding

1 (5.10-ounce) box instant vanilla pudding
    plus ingredients to prepare per directions on box
1 (8-ounce) tub Cool Whip
1 teaspoon vanilla flavoring
Bananas, how ever many your heart desires
1 box vanilla wafer cookies

This recipe is very special to me because it's my daddy's favorite desert, and he likes it best when I make it.

Prepare pudding per box directions. Stir in Cool Whip, vanilla and bananas. Set aside. Line the bottom and sides of a glass baking or serving dish with vanilla wafers. Pour pudding mix on top. Press more vanilla wafers around edges leaving them sticking out the top. Chill and Serve.

Angelia Johnson, Morton

Rice Pudding

1⅓ cups sugar
2 tablespoons flour
2 cups milk
4 eggs, beaten
4 tablespoons butter
1½ cups cooked rice
1 teaspoon vanilla

Mix sugar, flour, milk and eggs. Melt butter in a separate bowl. Add rice and vanilla; stir well. Combine 2 mixtures stirring well. Pour into pan. Bake at 350° until golden brown.

Joy Sumerall, Raymond

Mississippi Festivals

The following is a list of over 200 annual festivals found throughout the Magnolia State. Chances are we've neglected to include some events. If you are aware of any we missed, call us toll-free 1.888.854.5954, and we'll do our best to include it in a subsequent printing. Keep in mind, too, that dates and venues change. Please verify all information before making plans to attend any of these events. Festivals are listed alphabetically by the city where the festival is held. Please call the number listed or visit the festival's website for more information.

Aberdeen • Bukka White Bluff Festival
October • 662.369.9440 • bukkawhitefestival.com

Amory • Railroad Festival
April • 662.256.2761 • amoryrailroadfestival.com

Baldwyn • Okeelala Festival & Car Show
October • 662.365.1050 • cityofbaldwyn.com

**Bassfield • Prentiss Pickin' & Grinnin'
Bluegrass, Country & More Concert**
September • 601.792.5142 • jeffdavisms.com

raclro • Image from istockphoto.com

Batesville • SpringFest
May • 662.563.3126 • panolacounty.com

Bay Springs • Jazz in the Grove
April • 800.898.2782 • jazzinthegrove.net

Bay St. Louis • Bay BridgeFest
May • 228.467.9048 • hancockchamber.org

Bay St. Louis • Crab Festival
July • 228.467.6509 • olgchurch.net/crab.htm

Bay St. Louis • Krewe of Kids
February • 228.216.0506 • hancockchamber.org

**Bay St. Louis • Old Town Fall Fest & Jammin' Jambalaya
Cook Off**
October • 228.216.9045 • hancockchamber.org

Bay St. Louis • Our Lady of the Gulf Crab Festival
July • 228.467.6509 • olgchurch.net

Bay St. Louis • Paws on Parade & Pet Festival
March • 228.216.7387 • friendsoftheanimalshelter.org

Bay St. Louis • St. Rose de Lima Fair
October • 228.838.2806 or 228.467.7347
hancockchamber.org

Belmont • Bear Creek Festival & Antique Car Show
September • 662.454.0054 or 662.454.3381
mississippihills.org

Belzoni • World Catfish Festival
April • 662.247.4838 • worldcatfishfestival.org

Bentonia • Blues Festival
June • 662.746.1815 • yazoo.org

Biloxi • Beauvoir Fall Muster
October • 228.388.4400 • beauvoir.org

Biloxi • Billy Creel Memorial Wooden Boat Show
May • 228.435.6320 • maritimemuseum.org

Biloxi • Fais Do-Do & Blessing of the Fleet
June • 800.245.6943 or 228.435.6339 • biloxiblessing.com

Biloxi • Biloxi Seafood Festival
September • 228.604.0014 • biloxi.org

Biloxi • Chefs of the Coast
September • 228.236.1420 • chefsofthecoast.com

Biloxi • Coast Coliseum Summer Fair
June • 228.594.3700 • mscoastcoliseum.com

Biloxi • Cruisin the Coast
October • 888.808.1188 • cruisinthecoast.com

Biloxi • Cruisin' Keesler
September • 228.337.3160 • keeslerservices.org

Biloxi • George Ohr Fall Festival of Arts
October • 228.374.5547 • georgeohr.org

Biloxi • Great Biloxi Schooner Race
June • 228.435.6320 • maritimemuseum.org

Biloxi • Grillin' on the Green Spring Fling
March • 228.435.6339 • biloxi.ms.us

Biloxi • Gulf Coast Latin Festival
September • 228.365.7377

Biloxi • Mississippi Coast Coliseum Crawfish Festival
April • 800.726.2781 or 228.594.3700 • mscoastcoliseum.com

Biloxi • Mississippi Gulf Coast Bike Fest
April • 228.297.0256 • msbikefest.org

Biloxi • Puttin on the Roux!
October • 228.432.0301 • thebackbaymission.org

Biloxi • Scrapin the Coast
June • 228.832.2688 or 228.832.4683 • scrapinthecoast.com

Brandon • Brandon Day Festival
May • 601.825.5021 • cityofbrandon.net

Brookhaven • Annual Camellia Show
February • 800.613.4667 or 601.833.4126
brookhavenchamber.com

Brookhaven • Exchange Club Fair
July • 800.613.4667 • brookhavenchamber.com

Brookhaven • Ole Brook Festival
October • 800.613.4667 • brookhavenchamber.com

Bruce • Sawmill Festival
July • 662.983.2222

Burnsville • Waterway Festival
September • 662.427.9526 • burnsvillems.com

Byhalia • Clydesdale Christmas Store Fest
June • 662.838.8127 • clydesdalechristmasstore.org

Byhalia • White Oak Fall Festival
October • 901.246.8843

Byram • Swinging Bridge Festival
April • 601.371.0005 • byramswingingbridgefestival.com

Canton • Flea Market
May, October • 601.859,8055 • cantonmsfleamarket.com

Canton • Gospel Fest Homecoming
July • 601.859.1307 • cantontourism.com

Canton • Mississippi Championship Hot Air Balloon Race
July • 601.859.4358 • ballooncanton.com

Canton • Victorian Christmas Festival
November • 601.859.1307 • cantontourism.com

Carrollton • Carrollton Pilgrimage & Pioneer Day Festival
October • 662.237.6926 • CarrolltonMS.com

Carthage • The Square Affair
May • 601.267.9231 • leakems.com

Choctaw • Indian Fair
July • 601.656.1000 • choctawindianfair.com

Clarksdale • Caravan Music Fest
May • 901.605.8662 • blues2rock.com

Clarksdale • Cat Head Mini Festival
April • 662.624.5992 • cathead.biz

Clarksdale • Film Festival
January • 662.624.5992 • cathead.biz

Clarksdale • Delta Jubilee & Best Burger in the Delta Cook-Off
June • 662.627.7337 • clarksdale-ms.com

Clarksdale • Friday at the Stage
May • 800.626.3764 • clarksdale-ms.com

Clarksdale • Hambone Festival
October • 662.253.5586 • hambonefestival.com

Clarksdale • Juke Joint Festival
April • 662.624.5992 • jukejointfestival.com

Clarksdale • Mississippi Delta Tennessee Williams Festival
October • 662.627.7337 • ccc.cc.ms.us/twilliams

Clarksdale • Pinetop Perkins Homecoming
October • 662.902.3866 • hopsonplantation.com

Clarksdale • Sunflower River Blues & Gospel
August • 662.627.5301 • sunflowerfest.org

Cleveland • Crosstie Arts and Jazz Festival
April • 662.402.5451 • crosstie-arts.org

Cleveland • Italian Festival of Mississippi
March • 662.843.2712 • italianfestivalofmississippi.com

Cleveland • Octoberfest
October • 800.295.7473 • visitclevelandms.com

Collins • Okatoma Festival
May • 601.765.6012 • covingtonchamber.com

Collinsville • Gourd Gracious Farms Festival
September • 601.737.5333
gourdgracious.homestead.com/gourds.html

Columbia • Legends of Bluegrass & Country Music
October • 601.736.2550

Columbus • 7th Avenue Heritage Festival
January • 662.329.1191 • columbus-ms.org

Columbus • Artesia Days Festival
August • 662.272.5104 • columbus-ms.info

Columbus • Grilling on the River
April • 662.328.6850 • grillingontheriver.8m.net

Columbus • Heritage Festival
October • 662.329.1191 • columbus-ms.org

Columbus • Market Street Festival
May • 662.328.6305 • columbus-ms.org

Columbus • Roast N Boast
August • 662.549.5054 • roastnboast.com

Corinith • Celebrate Corinith
November • 662.287.1550 • corinth.ms

Corinth • Corinth Civil War Relic Show
March • 662.286.6779 • battleofcorinth.com

Corinth • Crossroad's Chilli Cookoff
April • 800.748.9048 • crossroadsfestival.corinth.net

Corinth • Hog Wild Festival
October • 662.287.1550 • hogwildfestival.com

Corinth • The Slugburger Festival
July • 662.287.1550 • slugburgerfestival.com

Crystal Springs • Crystal Springs Tomato Fest
June • 601.892.2711 • crystalspringsmiss.com

D'Iberville • BBQ Throwdown & Festival
February, March • 228.392.7966 • diberville.ms.us

Dennis • Dennis Day Music Fest
May • 662.293.0136 • mississippihills.org

Drew • Delta Wings Festival
November • 662.745.8975 • deltawingsfestival.com

Ellisville • Rotary Festival
November • 601.477.3323 • edajones.com

Enterprise • May Festival
May • 601.776.5701 • visitclarkecounty.com

Farmington • Heritage Festival & Battle of Farmington
September • 662.665.9647 • battleoffarmington.com

Forest • Wing Dang Doodle Festival
September • 601.469.4332 • forestareachamber.com

French Camp • Harvest Festival
October • 662.547.6482 • frenchcamp.org

French Camp • French Camp Pioneer Day
May • 662.547.9464 • frenchcamp.org

Gautier • Fall Festival
October • 228.497.8000 • gautier-ms.gov

Gautier • Gautier Mullet & Music Fest
October • 228.217.3152 • gautiermulletfest.com

Gluckstadt • German Festival
September • 601.856.2054 • stjosephgluckstadt.com

Greenville • Annual Catfish Races
May • 662.378.3121 • mainstreetgreenville.com

Greenville • Mississippi Delta Blues & Heritage Festival
September • 888.812.5837 • deltablues.org

Greenville • Mississippi Jazz & Heritage Festival
September • 662.247.3364 • jazzmississippi.com

Greenville • Native American Days
November • 662.334.4684

Greenwood • Mississippi Blues Fest
March • 662.453.4065 • mississippibluesfest.com

Greenwood • River to the Rails Festival
September • 662.453.7625 • mainstreetgreenwood.com

Greenwood • Stars and Stripes in the Park
June • 800.748.9064 or 662.453.4152 • greenwoodms.org

**Greenwood • The Roy Martin Delta Band
Festival Parade & Fireworks**
December • 800.748.9064 • greenwoodms.org

Grenada • Thunder on the Water Safeboarding Festival
June • 662.226.2571 • thunderonwater.net

Gulfport • Cajun, Country, Swamp Pop Music Festival
October • 228.547.7323

Gulfport • Margaritafest
June • 228.604.0014 • mscoastchamber.com

Gulfport • Memorial Day Blowout
May • 228.392.8281
gulfportmemorialdayblowout.com

Gulfport • Mississippi Navy Week
March • 228.871.2699 • navyweek.org

Gulfport • Scottish Games & Celtic Festival
November • 228.574.8218 • highlandsandislands.org

Gulfport • Seabee Day
March • 228.871.2699 • seabeeday.org

Hattiesburg • Dulcimer Festival
February • 601.583.6424 • mississippidulcimer.com

Hattiesburg • HUBFest
March • 800.238.4288 or 601.296.7500 • theADP.com

Hattiesburg • Mobile Street Renassiance Festival
October • 601.582.2560 • mobilestreetfestival.com

Hernando • A'Fair
May • 662.280.8875 • hernandooptimist.org

Hernando • Desoto Shrine Club BBQ Festival Cook Off
June • 662.890.3430 • desotobbq.com.

Hernando • Music & Heritage Festival
October • 662.429.9055 • hernandoms.org

Hernando • Love Music Festival
September • 662.429.2540 • lovemusicfest.com

Hernando • Museum Day Heritage Celebration
April • 662.429.8852 • desotomuseum.org

Holly Springs • Kudzu Festival
July • 888.687.4765 • visithollysprings.com

Holly Springs • Strawberry Plains Festival
September • 662.252.1155 • strawberryplains.audubon.org

Horn Lake • Autumn in the Park
October • 662.781.4529 • hornlake.org

Horn Lake • Independence Celebration
July • 662.781.4529 • hornlakeparks.com

Houston • Fall Flywheel Festival
September • 662.456.2321 • houstonms.org/fly

Iuka • Heritage Festival
September • 866.807.6020 or 662.423.3954

Jackson • Bright Lights, Belhaven Nights
August • 601.352.8850 • greaterbelhaven.com

Jackson • CelticFest Mississippi
September • 601.713.3365 • celticfestms.org

Mississippi

Jackson • Chimneyville Crafts Festival
December • 601.856.7546 • mscraftsmenguild.org

Jackson • Crossroads Film Festival
April • 601.510.9148 • crossroadsfilmfestival.com

Jackson • Farish Street Heritage Festival
September • 601.948.5667 • farishstfestival.com

Jackson • Mal's St. Paddy's Parade and Festival
March • 601.984.1972 • halandmals.com

Jackson • Mississippi Performing Arts Festival
March • 601.977.9840 • mspuppetry.com

Jackson • Mississippi State Fair
October • 601.278.4513 • mdac.state.ms.us

Jackson • NatureFEST!
April • 601.354.7303 • msnaturalscience.org

Jackson • Sweetheart Squaredancing Festival
March • 662.871.7581 • mssquaredance.com

Jackson • Trail of Honor
May • 601.372.5770 • trailofhonor.org

Kosciusko • Natchez Trace Festival
April • 662.289.2981 • kadcorp.org/NTF.asp

Laurel • Day in the Park
May • 601.649.6374 • laurelartsleague.com

Laurel • Lauren Rogers Museum of Art Blues Bash
June • 601.649.6374 • lrma.org

Laurel • Loblolly Festival
October • 601.433.3255 • loblollyfestival.com

Laurel • Mother's Day Blues Festival
May • 734.994.0138 • laurelms.com

Laurel • South Mississippi Fair
October • 601.649.9010 • southmissfair.com

Leland • Highway 61 Blues Festival
June • 662.686.7646 • highway61blues.com

Leland • Leland Crawfish Festival
May • 662.347.4223 • highway61blues.com

Lizana • St. Ann's Catfish Festival
May • 228.832.2560 • catholic-church.org/stann/fish

Long Beach • Long Beach Fest
August • 228.234-6622 • longbeachfest.com

Long Beach • Mississippi Gulf Coast Kite Festival
May • 228.604.0014 • mscoastchamber.com

Long Beach • Southern Miss Jazz & Blues Festival
April • 228.865.4573 • usm.edu/gc/jazz-n-blues

Lucedale • The Gingham Tree Arts and Crafts Festival
November • 601.947.2755 • georgecounty.ms

Macon • Dancing Rabbit Festival
October • 662.726.4456 • noxubeecounty.org

Madison • A Day in the Country
October • 601.856.2593 • chapelofthecrossms.org

Madison • Grillin' for Life
October • 601.214.9463 • grillinforlife.com

Magee • Crazy Day
September • 601.849.2517 • mageechamberofcommerce.com

McComb • Pike County Azalea Festival
March • 601.684.2291 • pikeinfo.com

Meridian • Jimmie Rodgers Memorial Festival
May • 601.693.1361 • jimmierodgers.com

Meridian • Soule' Live Steam Festival - Railfest
November • 601.917.3471 • soulelivesteam.com

Mize • Watermelon Festival
July 23 & 24 • 601.733.5647 • mswatermelonfestival.com

Monticello • Atwood Music Festival
May • 601.587.3007 • atwoodmusicfestival.com

Moss Point • Moss Point River Festival
October • 228.388.2323

Mize Watermelon Festival

Moss Point • Old Time River Jamboree
May • 228.475.7887

Moss Point • Pascagoula River Nature Festival
April • 228.475.0825 • pascagoularivernaturefestival.com

Mound Bayou • Founder's Day
July • 662.741.2194 • cityofmoundbayou.org

Mound Bayou • Mississippi Delta Children's Literacy Festival
September • 662.741.2683 • mbpsaa.org

Natchez • Great Mississippi River Balloon Race
October • 601.446.6345 • natchezballoonrace.com

Natchez • Juneteenth Celebration
June • 601.445.0728 • visitnatchez.org

Natchez • Natchez Bluff Blues Festival
April • 601.442.0814 • visitnatchez.org

Natchez • Natchez Festival of Music
May • 601..442.7464
natchezfestivalofmusic.art.officelive.com

Natchez • Natchez Food & Wine Festival
July • 601.446.6631 • natchezfoodandwinefest.com

Natchez • Natchez Literary & Cinema Celebration
February • 866.296.6522 • colin.edu/nlcc

Natchez • Natchez Powwow
March • 601.446.6502 • natchezpowwow.com

New Albany • Tallahatchie River Fest
September • 662.534.4354 • tallahatchieriverfest.com

Newton • Loose Caboose Festival
March • 601.683.2201 • newtonmschamber.com

Newton • Wildlife Festival
September • 662.325.3174 • naturalresources.msstate.edu

Ocean Springs • Herb and Garden Fest
March• 228.875.4424 • oceanspringschamber.com

Ocean Springs • 1699 Landing of D'Iberville Arts & Crafts Festival
April • 228.875.7008 • 1699landing.org

Ocean Springs • Battle on the Bayou
March • 228.872.2030 • battleonthebayou.com

Ocean Springs • Feast of Flavors - Taste the Town!
September • 228.875.4424 or 228.257.2496
oceanspringschamber.com

Ocean Springs • Mayfest
May • 228.818.9885 • gulfcoast.org

Ocean Springs • Ocean Springs Kayak Festival
June • 228.872.2030 • southcoastpaddling.com

Ocean Springs • Peter Anderson Memorial Arts, Crafts & Food Festival
November • 228.875.1032 • oceanspringschamber.com

Ocean Springs • Red, White, & Blueberry Festival
June • 228.875.4424 • oceanspringschamber.com

Ocean Springs • Shed BBQ Shedhead Blues Festival
September • 228.875.9590 • theshedbbq.com

Ocean Springs • Taste of Ocean Springs Food & Wine Festival
May • 228.875.4424 • oceanspringschamber.com

Olive Branch • OctoberFest
October • 662.893.5219 • obms.us

Oxford • Blues Festival
July • 769.226.5736 • oxfordbluesfest.com

Oxford • Double Decker Arts Fest
April • 662.234.4680 • doubledeckerfestival.com

Oxford • Shakespeare Festival
June - July • 662.915.5745 • shakespeare.olemiss.edu

Oxford • Yocona International Folk Fest
August • 662.801.3438 • yoconafestival.org

Pascagoula • Blues & Heritage Festival
September • 228.497.5493 • msgulfcoastbluesfest.com

Pascagoula • Live Oaks Arts Festival
April • 228.938.6604 • cityofpascagoula.com

Pascagoula • Sounds by the Sea
May • 228.938.6604 • gulfcoastsymphony.net

Pascagoula • Zonta Club Art & Crafts Festival
October • 228.762.7018 • zontapascagoula.info

Pass Christian • Art in the Pass
April • 228.452.2360 • artinthepass.com

Pass Christian • Christmas in the Pass & Boat Parade
December • 228.604.0014 • passchamber.com

Pass Christian • Rockin' the Globe
May • 228.467.9057 • ststan.com

Pass Christian • St. Paul's Seafood Festival
June • 228.596.1896 • seafood.passchristian.net

Pearl • Pearl Day
May • 601.932.3541 • cityofpearl.com

Pelahatchie • Muscadine Jubilee
September • 601.854.5224 • pelahatchie.org

Philadelphia • Ham Jam Arts Festival
April • 601.656.1000 • hamjamartsfestival.com

Picayune • Picayune Fall Street Fair
November • 601.799.3070 • picayunemainstreet.com

Picayune • Spring Street Fair
April • 601.799.3070 • picayunemainstreet.com

Pontotoc • Bodock Festival
August • 662.489.5042 • pontotocchamber.com

Poplarville • The Blueberry Jubilee
June • 601.759.8377 • blueberryjubilee.org

Potts Camp • North Mississippi Hill Country Picnic
June • 662.252.2515 • nmshillcountrypicnic.com

Quitman • Clarke County Forestry and Wildlife Festival
September • 601.776.5701 • VisitClarkeCounty.com

Raleigh • Raleigh Heritage Festival
September • 601.782.4527 • smithcounty.ms.gov

Raymond • Raymond Country Fair
May • 601.857.8942 • raymondms.com

Richland • Richland Day
October • 601.420.3400 • richlandms.com

Richton • Mississippi Pecan Festival
September • 601.964.8201 • mspecanfestival.com

Ridgeland • Celebrate America Balloon Glow
July • 601.853.2011 • ridgelandms.org

Ridgeland • KidFest Ridgeland
April • 601.853.2011 • visitridgeland.com

Ridgeland • Renaissance Fine Arts Festival
May • 601.605.5252 • visitridgeland.com

Rolling Fork • Deep Delta Festival
April • 662.873.4353 • deepdelta.org

Rolling Fork • Great Delta Bear Affair
October • 662.873.6261 • greatdeltabearaffair.org

Rosedale • Crossroads Blues & Heritage Festival
May • 800.295.7473 or 662.843.6110
rosedaleblues.com

Senatobia • Mayfair
May • 662.562.8715 • tate-county.com

Southaven • Creole Crawfish Festival
April • 901.619.5865 • creolecrawfishfestival.com

Southaven • Springfest
April • 662.280.2489 • southavenspringfest.com

Southaven • Tri-State Blues Festival
August • 662.280.9120

Stonewall • Come Home to Stonewall Day
October • 601.659.3080 • visitclarkecounty.com

Sturgis • Sturgis South All-Bike Motorcyle Rally
August • 662.465.7970 • sturgismsrally.com

Taylorsville • Grillin' and Chillin' BBQ Festival
November • 601.785.4756 • smithcounty.ms.gov

Tishomingo • Archie Lee Memorial Dulcimer Festival
October • 662.438.6914

Tishomingo • Hollis Long Memorial Dulcimer Festival
April • 662.438.6914

Tunica • Delta Day Festival
October • 662.363.6611 • tunicamainstreet.com

Tunica • Mid-South Fair
September • 901.274.8800 • midsouthfair.com

Tunica • Rivergate Festival
April • 662.363.2865 • tunicachamber.com

Tunica • Wild Game Cook-Off
February • 662.363.6611 • tunicamainstreet.com

Tupelo • Dudies Burger Festival
May • 662.841.6438 • orendunnmuseum.org

Tupelo • Elvis Presley Festival
June • 662.841.6598 • tupeloelvisfestival.com

Tupelo • Gum Tree Festival
May • 662.844.2787 • gumtreemuseum.com

Tupelo • Presley Heights Azalea Festival
April • 800.533.0611 or 662.841.6521
presleyheights.com

Tupelo • Blue Suede Cruise
May • 1.800.533.0611 • bluesc.com

Tupelo • Film Festival
May • 662.841.6521 • tupelofilmfestival.net

Tylertown • Bluegrass on the Creek
May • 601.876.5606 • walthallchamber.com/bluegrass.

Tylertown • Dairy Festival
June • 601.876.2680 • walthallchamber.com/dairyfest

Vancleave • Bluff Creek Bluegrass Festival
May • 228.8263.1179 or 228.217.9688
bluffcreekbluegrass.com

Vancleave • Ole Time Festival & Mule Pull
March • 228.826.3019 or 228.219.6301 • smmha.com

Vardaman • Sweet Potato Festival
November • 662.682.7559
vardamansweetpotatofestival.org

Vicksburg • Alcorn State University Jazz Festival
April • 1.800.822.6338 or 601.630.2929 • alcorn.edu/jazzfest

Vicksburg • Riverfest
April • 601.634.4527 • riverfestms.com

**Washington • Copper Magnolia
Fine Arts & Crafts Festival**
September • 601.442.2901 • mdah.state.ms.us

Water Valley • Watermelon Carnival
August • 662.473.1122 • watervalleychamber.info

Waveland • Krewe of Nereids
February • 1.800.466.9048 or 228.463.9222
visitmississippi.org

Waveland • Waveland Oyster Fest
April • 228.467.0855 • wavelandcommunitycoalition.com

West Point • Howlin' Wolf Memorial Blues Festival
September • 662.605.0770 • wpnet.org/Howlin_Festival.htm

West Point • Pràrie Arts Festival
September • 662.494.5121 • wpnet.org

Wiggins • Pine Hill Festival
April • 601.928.5418 • stonecounty.com

Yazoo City • Jerry Clower Festival
May • 662.746.7676 • yazoo.org

Yazoo City • Yazoo County Fair
October • 662.746.1815 • yazoo.org

Index

Eat & Explore State Cookbook Series

Experience our United States like never before when you explore the distinct flavor of each state by savoring 250 favorite recipes from the state's best cooks. In addition, the state's favorite events and destinations are profiled throughout the book with fun stories and everything you need to know to plan your family's next road trip.

- Eat & Explore Arkansas
- Eat & Explore Minnesota
- Eat & Explore North Carolina
- Eat & Explore Ohio

- Eat & Explore Oklahoma
- Eat & Explore Virginia
- Eat & Explore Washington

EACH: $18.95 • 240 TO 272 PAGES • 7x9 • PAPERBOUND • FULL-COLOR

State Back Road Restaurants Cookbook Series

From two-lane highways and interstates, to dirt roads and quaint downtowns, every road leads to delicious food when traveling across our United States. The brand-new State Back Road Restaurants Cookbook Series serves up a well-researched and charming guide to each state's best back road restaurants. No time to travel? No problem. Each restaurant shares with you their favorite recipes— sometimes their signature dish, sometimes a family favorite, but always delicious. This outstanding new series brings you terrific recipes plus a guide to those restaurants you won't want to miss while traveling the back roads. So crank up your car and join the fun.

- Alabama Back Road Restaurant Recipes
- Kentucky Back Road Restaurant Recipes
- Tennessee Back Road Restaurant Recipes
- Texas Back Road Restaurant Recipes

EACH: $18.95 • 256 PAGES • 7x9 • PAPERBOUND • FULL-COLOR

www.GreatAmericanPublishers.com • www.facebook.com/GreatAmericanPublishers

Hometown Cookbook

State Hometown Cookbook Series

A Hometown Taste of America, One State at a Time

EACH: **$18.95** • **240 to 272 pages** • **8x9** • **paperbound**

The STATE HOMETOWN COOKBOOK SERIES captures each state's hometown charm by combining great-tasting local recipes from real hometown cooks with interesting stories and photos from festivals all over the state. As a souvenir, gift, or collector's item, this unique series is sure to take you back to your hometown... or take you on a journey to explore other hometowns across the country.

- Easy to follow recipes produce great-tasting dishes every time.
- Recipes use ingredients you probably already have in your pantry.
- Fun-to-read sidebars feature food-related festivals across the state.
- The perfect gift for anyone who loves to cook.

- Georgia Hometown Cookbook
- Louisiana Hometown Cookbook
- Mississippi Hometown Cookbook
- South Carolina Hometown Cookbook
- Tennessee Hometown Cookbook
- Texas Hometown Cookbook
- West Virginia Hometown Cookbook

------ ✂ — — — —

Order Form MAIL TO: Great American Publishers • 171 Lone Pine Church Road • Lena, MS 39094

Qty.	Title	Total
	Subtotal	
	Postage ($4 first book; $1 each additional) (order 4 or more for free postage)	
	Total	

☐ Check Enclosed

Charge to: ☐ Visa ☐ MC ☐ AmEx ☐ Disc

Card# _____

Exp Date _____ Signature _____

Name _____

Address _____

City _____ State _____ Zip _____

Phone _____

Email _____